ADVICE FROM THE TOP

1001 BITS OF BUSINESS WISDOM FROM THE GREAT LEADERS OF THE RECENT PAST

EDITED BY

DEL LEONARD JONES

Table of Contents

Foreword

Chief executive officers and football coaches have much in common. For one, they field unusual questions from the business and sports media. The oddest question ever posed to me came in 2006 when I was CEO of TD Ameritrade. Del Jones of *USA Today* asked if I was spanked as a child.

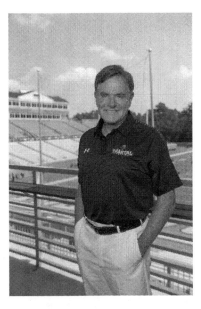

I have this curious habit of giving honest answers. I told him I was hit once a month when things were going well and once a week when things weren't. My parents were hardworking immigrants, who didn't like to find out I was somewhere I wasn't supposed to be. They didn't like me in fistfights — unless someone else started it.

I picked up *USA Today* to find out that Del had directed the same question to twenty CEOs. Rick Wagoner of General Motors had received occasional "whacks in the fanny," but said he probably deserved more. Leggett & Platt's Dave Haffner confessed to Del that he was familiarized with his father's belt about six times a year, including the time he kicked down the door after his brother locked him in the basement. Mark Cuban got the "this is going to hurt me more than it hurts you," speech from his dad. The mother of General Electric's Jack Welch whacked him with a shoe if he skipped altar-boy practice.

Del made a name for himself reporting such offbeat stories about business leaders. One was about cheating at golf. No CEO confessed, but each one had witnessed other CEOs cheating the game. Another of Del's stories was about CEOs who had near-death experiences, including Micron Technology's Steve Appleton, who had survived a stunt plane crash in 2004.

"Kids who are 18 think they will live forever," Appleton told Del. "They take huge risks when they have their entire lives ahead of them. When George Bush went skydiving at 80, they made a big deal. The older you get, the more risk you should take."

Three years after the interview, Appleton died when a plane he built from a kit crashed after takeoff. Pilot error was blamed.

Del started writing unorthodox stories when *USA Today* decided it needed more CEOs to read the newspaper. The reason was clear. They heavily influenced advertising decisions and executives, especially New York executives, had their noses buried in the *Wall Street Journal* and the *New York Times*. Del was given the corporate leadership beat to lure them into *USA Today* – and not just when they were traveling.

Del chose to write stories of interest to executives, but he also wanted his work to appeal to *USA Today*'s more populist readership of NASCAR and Hollywood enthusiasts. Whatever he did worked. *USA Today* published more than 300 of his cover stories and nominated him for a Pulitzer Prize in beat reporting. He also wrote a monthly Q&A called Advice from the Top and interviewed the best-known CEOs of the time including Cuban, Xerox's Anne Mulcahy, and Michael Dell. Their wisdom is boiled down in this book, which is a quick read for the busy. Don't miss the lessons of history from FedEx's Fred Smith.

Del's Advice from the Top Q&A became coveted real estate and he insisted that CEOs offer useful advice. He wouldn't let them get away with mere promotion. For example, when Jack Welch had a book out and wanted to sell it, Del wouldn't interview him until he agreed to talk about his controversial policy of firing the bottom 10% of GE employees each year.

Some of the best business advice in the pages that follow came from successful people outside the corporate world, such as musicians Wynton Marsalis and Lorin Maazel, game show host Howie Mandel and astronaut Sally Ride, who died in 2012.

Just before Super Bowl XXXIX, I gave an interview to Del about the football lessons that apply to business. He came to me because I'd been a high school and college football coach for 16 years and had written the book *The Key to Winning Football: The Perimeter Attack Offense* before I went into broker training at Merrill Lynch in 1984.

Here are a few X's and O's from my interview with Del:

- ✓ Be sure your people are playing in the right positions.

- ✓ Know the odds of success and the consequence of failure when taking a risk.

✓ Ingenious game plans fail if no one is blocking and tackling.

✓ Success requires spiritual soundness, dedication, courage and love. Love is the willingness to sacrifice for the team. It doesn't matter how many points you score if the team loses.

I left as CEO of TD Ameritrade in 2008 and became head football coach of Coastal Carolina in 2012. As I hurriedly write this, my team is preparing for the 2018 opener against South Carolina. My teams are 51-15 and have played well enough to win for me the Eddie Robinson FCS National Coach of the Year and an induction into the Vince Lombardi Hall of Fame. I'm the subject of the Monte Burke book, *Fourth and Goal: One Man's Quest to Recapture His Dream.*

A great deal of business leadership advice can be gleaned from sports figures as you will discover in *Advice From the Top: 1001 Bits of Business Wisdom From the Great Leaders of the Recent Past.* Del interviewed Ronnie Lott and Steve Young of the San Francisco 49ers, NBA Coach Larry Brown, Indy driver Bobby Unser, poker professional Annie Duke, and Mike Eruzione, captain of the "Do you believe in miracles?" Olympic hockey team.

Del has just published the timely historical novel *The Cremation of Sam McGee* set in the 1898 heyday of yellow journalism. The main character is a New York reporter who fabricates stories from the Spanish-American War in Cuba to boost circulation. That's one reporter who deserved a spanking. Request the first chapter at:

https://caseystrikesout.wixsite.com/website).

Here are 1001 bits of wisdom. Some will not apply to your business. Many will and many will apply to your life. My one team rule as football coach of Coastal Carolina: Be A Man — better known in the locker room as "BAM." I ask my student-athletes to stand on their own two feet and take responsibility for their actions.

--Joe Moglia

Don't give lip service

— Duane Ackerman, BellSouth CEO 1997-2006 on customer complaints

- ✓ No matter who you are, when a customer complaint rises to your level, you own it until it gets fixed.

- ✓ Know how many complaints per 1,000 customers your company receives. Know how it's trending? Use an unbiased third party to track it.

- ✓ Customer surveys should be quick, never a hassle.

- ✓ Some customers are so difficult they're worth sending to a competitor.

"Remember, it costs more to get a new customer than to hold onto one."

- ✓ Airlines know that customers book the lowest fare. They won't often pay for better service. If that's the case in your industry, don't promise everything, manage expectations, but strive to live up to what's promised.

Did you know?

- Ackerman has a physics degree from Rollins College and an MBA from Massachusetts Institute of Technology.

- Year after year, BellSouth had the highest rating for customer service among local phone service providers.

Real men win 6-love, 6-love

— Steve Appleton, Micron Technology CEO 1994-2012 on the leadership lessons of tennis

- ✓ Tennis is superior to golf. It's better exercise and takes less time. Golf is overrated as a lubricant for business transactions.

"You don't wander around the woods looking for a ball that suddenly shows up. I can't stand people who cheat."

- ✓ A dishonest opponent in sports is likely to be dishonest in business.

- ✓ A tennis player behind 5-0 will conserve energy for the next set. Likewise, business leaders decide where to apply resources and where to do battle.

- ✓ Don't play it safe. If the only goal is to avoid mistakes, move to Japan.

"I played a customer from a Japanese company who thought he was really good. I beat him 6-0, 6-0. I wouldn't want anybody losing points to me on purpose."

✓ Sit back and wait and be eaten alive.

✓ Roger Federer hits winner after winner, but he's smart about it. He studies his opponents. Micron has employees who do nothing but look at the data and products of competitors.

✓ Small start-ups go for broke. Big, successful companies have the resources to be bold, but tend to play it safe. That doesn't make sense.

"When George Bush went skydiving at 80, they made a big deal. What if his parachute didn't open? So what? It's not like the guy hasn't done anything with his life. The older you get, the more risk you should take."

✓ Focus less on winning or losing. Focus on what it takes to win or lose.

✓ Don't teach children to be good losers. Life is not fair. Winning at all costs is a relative phrase, but definitely tell kids to go out and win.

✓ Temper tantrums are OK for the young, but not for an experienced executive in a leadership role.

✓ Tell employees to win. Explain the strategy. Get them to understand what must be accomplished.

✓ The business world moves fast but it's in slow motion compared to tennis. Don't panic.

Did you know?

- Appleton played tennis at Boise State and on the satellite professional circuit.

- Played a tiebreaker in college and lost three straight points to lose the match. He beat the head off of five wood rackets against a post. The wood was swept from the court with a broom.

"I didn't hurt anybody, I didn't scream at anybody. I didn't offend anybody. They might have thought I was nuts. It's a sign of immaturity."

- Started with Micron Technology in 1983 at $4.46 an hour. Became CEO in 1994 at age 34, the third-youngest Fortune 500 CEO at that time.

- Owned more than 20 airplanes and flew aerobatics. Crashed in July 2004 when his stunt plane stalled 25 feet off the ground. Saved his life with a last-second left rudder adjustment that elevated the plane's right wing.

- Died in 2012 when a plane he built from a kit crashed after takeoff in Boise. Pilot error was blamed.

"Kids who are 18 think they will live forever and take huge risk. They have their entire lives ahead of them. If I were to die tomorrow, I have no complaints. I've experienced more than anybody should expect in a lifetime."

Enrich debate inside the company

— Steve Baum, Sempra Energy CEO 1998-2006 on workplace diversity

- ✓ Strive not just for diversity of race, ethnicity and sex, but a diversity of point of view and perspective. It's a competitive advantage.

"We're not Noah's Ark. We don't need two of each."

- ✓ Shareholders aren't interested in diversity. Explain to them the role of workforce composition.

- ✓ Diversify in a slow economy when it's easier to find good workers.

"Skin color or sexual preference won't get you promoted. Performance will."

- ✓ Lawsuits don't go away when a company diversifies. They increase, an unintended consequence of doing the right thing.

✓ The culture must also change, or women and minority groups will become discouraged and sue where they otherwise wouldn't.

✓ Can't find qualified workers? A reputation as a welcoming company enhances recruitment of the best minorities and women. Most don't want to be the first to crack the all-white, male barrier where they may have to constantly fight the fight.

Did you know?

- Baum was a Marine Corps captain.

- Competed in high school football, wrestling and crew.

- Hobbies include cooking, wine collecting and hunting.

- Studied French and German in school, but learned Spanish well enough to do TV interviews and negotiate contracts in Mexico.

King of the hill

— **Steve Bennett, Intuit CEO 2000-07 on how to maintain dominance in an industry.**

- ✓ Never be a good loser. Be a good learner. Focus on unmet opportunities.

- ✓ Intel's Andy Grove was right, only the paranoid survive.

"Understand the real reason why you're losing share and respond intelligently. Too often, leaders cut prices. They take two aspirin without knowing what the illness is."

- ✓ Happy customers create a barrier to entry. They won't switch for a lower price, only for a superior product at a lower price.

- ✓ Keep an eye on competitors, but ultimately the company that delivers for customers wins.

- ✓ Business is not a Pop Warner football game. It's OK to run up the score.

Did you know?

- Bennett played baseball at the University of Wisconsin. Golf handicap: 5. Favorite course: Lake Course at the Olympic Club in San Francisco.

- Collects wine. Favorite: Amarone from Italy.

- Became CEO after 23 years at General Electric. Intuit revenue grew from $801 million in 1999 to $2 billion in 2005. Quicken personal finance software had a 70% market share, TurboTax had a 79% share, QuickBooks, had an 87% share despite repeated intrusions by Microsoft.

Don't be a scold

— Larry Brown, NBA and Olympic basketball coach on positive coaching

✓ Strive for a high ratio of positive-to-negative comments.

✓ Explain to players/workers you're trying to teach, not criticize. Be sincere when you tell them you want them to reach their potential.

✓ When they trust you're on their side, then correct them. That's coaching.

✓ No player/worker thrives on intimidation or shame.

✓ Don't hire people unless you believe in them.

✓ Recruit "A" players with great character. Reward them with money, but they must be part of the team. Great NBA players get more public adulation, but they must be good teammates or there are problems in the locker room. Likewise, hire "A" employees who don't need to be treated like prima donnas.

"If your best player has great character, the chances of succeeding are incredible. If your best player is not of good character, then you have a problem."

- Give pep talks. Tell the team to play hard, play together, play smart, and have fun.

- Win by maximizing everybody's talent.

- Tell them they don't win as individuals. They win by being unselfish and doing their jobs.

- Put people in an environment where they can be successful.

"Getting beat doesn't mean failure. When I was at the University of Kansas we lost five straight and ended up winning the championship."

✓ Don't play it safe. Accept mistakes are a part of taking the risk to win.

✓ There are different kinds of mistakes. Mistakes for lack of effort are bad. Mistakes for fear of losing are bad. Mistakes from giving best effort are good.

✓ Take the blame when the team screws up. Give them credit when they do well.

Did you know?

- Brown never had a regular job. He says that coaching is the only thing he could do. Enshrined into the Basketball Hall of Fame 2002.

- Joined the advisory board of the Positive Coaching Alliance after his 8-year-old son was screamed at by a youth baseball manager.

- His 2004 Detroit Pistons won the NBA championship months before his U.S. Olympic team limped home with a bronze medal. He said he was proud of both teams.

Inching towards perfection

— Lewis Campbell, Textron CEO 1998-2009 on Six Sigma

- ✓ Change will be resisted. Expect people to be content with the way things are.

- ✓ The work will seem harder until you get traction. Persist. You must be "all in."

- ✓ Six Sigma fails when it's used as a "Hail Mary" pass.

- ✓ Define a problem, take measurements to be crystal clear on what needs to improve, analyze the data using statistical tools to sort through the noise.

- ✓ Don't backslide. Once something is fixed, make sure it's fixed for the last time.

- ✓ The Six Sigma goal is three defects per million.

- ✓ Apply it to service departments, such as legal, as much as to manufacturing.

✓ Use it to let employees question the boss about how they manage. Challenge leadership with irrefutable data.

"Somebody out there has to be the premier company. Why can't we?"

✓ Resist the urge to pull key people out of training.

✓ Don't leap to help customers eliminate waste until Six Sigma is ingrained at your company.

Did you know?

- Campbell's an avid fly fisherman. Also skis and scuba dives.

- Six Sigma falls in and out of favor. It was introduced by Motorola engineer Bill Smith in 1986. Jack Welch embraced it at General Electric in 1995. It lost steam in the late 1990s. Campbell resuscitated it in 2003 when Textron's stock took a nosedive. By 2006, the stock had climbed to an all-time high.

Old dogs must learn new tricks

— John Chambers, Cisco Systems CEO 1995-2015 on embracing technology

- ✓ It's not more difficult to learn technology when you grow older. It's how you approach life.

- ✓ Geezers don't need to be geeks. Learn technology from a practical business approach.

- ✓ It's OK if you're not gadget-savvy. That's irrelevant. Figure out how to use technology to get closer to customers. Look for new market opportunities, get quick feedback. Gain advantage.

- ✓ Ask the geeks to quit using jargon.

- ✓ Be honest with engineers. Say, "I really didn't understand what you said. Can you explain it in terms that I can grasp?"

- ✓ Spend time with people who know technology better than yourself. Listen to them, make them teach you something.

Did you know?

- Chambers graduated near the top of his high school class despite having dyslexia.

- First job out of college was selling million-dollar mainframe computers at IBM. They didn't have the processing power of today's phones.

Doing business with the Red Dragon

— John Chen, Sybase CEO 1998-2010 on China

- ✓ China will stop stealing intellectual property once its middle class grows. Hong Kong, Singapore and Taiwan all graduated from rampant pirating. History runs its course.

"Japan took our cars and TVs apart to make them better. Even the United States stole writings from Charles Dickens in the 1800s. The Chinese are proud, they'd rather not be labeled as copycats."

- ✓ Resist protectionist urges. Hiring American restricts companies to 5% of the potential talent pool.

- ✓ In times of controversy, companies must strive to be neutral. Thread the political needle and move on.

- ✓ English remains the international language of business, but knowing Mandarin will prove more valuable than learning Japanese in the 1980s. Japan's economy was never open, so the opportunity lost wasn't as great.

Did you know?

- Chen was born in Hong Kong. His parents escaped communism in Shanghai and moved to Massachusetts.

- Testified before Congress on U.S.-China trade relations. Served on President George W. Bush's export council.

- Governor of San Francisco Symphony. Favorite composers: Mendelssohn, Tchaikovsky.

No balls, no babies

— Mark Cuban, Self-made billionaire on risky business

- ✓ Go for it when you have nothing. If you lose, you still have nothing.

- ✓ Don't borrow, especially from friends and family. Lose your money, not other people's. Accept 100% of the risk and reward of any new venture.

- ✓ Fear of failure forces you to prepare.

- ✓ If preparation tells you that risk-aversion is the right way to get results, be risk-averse.

"When the opportunity arises, most people don't have the courage to go for it."

- ✓ Business is Darwinian. If you go broke you get to start over as a more evolved entrepreneur.

- ✓ Find something you love. If you don't make money at it, at least you like going to work.

- ✓ In business deals, look for the fool. If you don't see one, the fool is you.

Did you know?

- Cuban first heard "no balls, no babies" from a blackjack dealer in Las Vegas.

- Got rich launching tech companies.

- First job was selling garbage bags door to door at age 12.

- He owns the Dallas Mavericks. First dunked a basketball at age 37.

- Best sports bar in any NBA city: Kilroy's in Bloomington, Ind.

- Advises small investors to stay out of the stock market and put their savings in a bank. Favorite book: *The Number* by Alex Berenson, about how corporate fraud is driven by Wall Street's focus on quarterly earnings.

When it rains it pours

— Michael Dell, Dell Computer founder and CEO on thriving in hard times

- ✓ Don't focus on stock price. Focus on things you can control such as costs and product mix. Through good days and bad, worry about building a company.

- ✓ As more and more customers order directly, let them tell you what they want and need. If you listen, they'll tell you where to go next, where to expand.

"Let customers order what they want. Don't try to get them to buy what you've made."

- ✓ Customers want flexibility and value. Whoever provides it will win.

- ✓ Ask: what do customers most want us to do next? Do it, then learn quickly if it's a dud or a winner.

- ✓ Get insiders off your board. Independent directors not only keep the company honest, they help it succeed with outside ideas.

- ✓ Be known as a prestigious place to work. Get people beating down the door to join your company.

- ✓ Find out where competitors are making too much money off a product. That's where opportunity lies.

- ✓ When capital dries up, big companies are in a better position to score on new products. Reach out to those who are working out of their garages. Let them be part of your R&D ecosystem.

Did you know?

- Dell was a pre-med major at the University of Texas. He dropped out at 19. His only business course was macroeconomics.

"My parents were very upset until I showed them my first financial statement."

- Owned a BMW at age 16 after targeting newspaper subscriptions to newlyweds.

- Pre-Zuckerberg, Dell was the youngest-ever CEO of a Fortune 500 company at 27 and a billionaire at 31. By 34, he was richer than Bill Gates at the same age.

Roll up your sleeves

— Bob Dickinson, Carnival Cruise Lines CEO 2003-07 on grunt work

- ✓ Listen to front-line employees. They know their jobs far better than you.

- ✓ Don't come down from the mountain with tablets of stone. Be the most humble around your company's lowest-paid.

- ✓ Focus on the needs of employees, especially those who are face to face with your customers.

- ✓ Do your grunt workers a big favor by managing customer expectations. Don't advertise your product as luxury or gourmet unless it is. The hard-working front-line workers will absorb the blame for any shortfall.

"We challenge the marketing department to create the lowest level of expectations but just high enough for customers to buy the product."

✓ There are more productive places for top leadership to spend time than in the trenches.

Did you know?

- Dickinson was the first to appear on the PBS program Back to the Floor. He worked five jobs on a cruise from Miami to the Caribbean including maid service.

- Says he'd rather be CEO for minimum wage than a cabin maid for $3 million in salary, bonus and restricted stock.

"If you've been the conductor, you don't want to be first violin anymore."

- Had never seen a cruise ship until he went on a job interview at Carnival. He was once seasick on a sailboat. There was "no loss of fluids."

- Were he forced to do karaoke on a cruise ship, he would sing American Pie.

- Trench jobs he's worked include pumping gas in Pittsburgh and selling industrial tires.

Offshoring is not a dirty word

— Uwe Doerken, DHL executive chairman 2004-08 on outsourcing jobs to foreign countries

- ✓ Don't feel guilty. Offshoring and outsourcing benefit the consumer and the world economy.

- ✓ Outsourcing doesn't hurt first-world economies. Efficient and less costly production leads to affordable products and services that allow the first-world to stay competitive.

- ✓ Encourage your country or community to establish clusters of expertise. Those clusters keep good jobs and attract new ones.

"It's about adapting and keeping the highest value-added jobs."

- ✓ Over time, expect economies to move up the skill curve. What was a high-skill job yesterday becomes a medium skill today and low skill tomorrow. Sewing was high-tech in the 19th century. It has migrated to India, China and now to other Asian countries.

✓ Education is continuous. It's no longer enough to learn a trade for life.

✓ Convince governments not to tax or otherwise punish companies trying to produce more affordable products and services.

✓ Don't fear backlash. Educate.

Did you know?

- Doerken was born in Schwelm, Germany. Fluent in English, German, French, Spanish and Dutch.

- Rides a Harley along coastal and mountain roads.

- Slept in a different bed, on average, every third night.

- Favorite travel destination: Thailand, with its natural beauty, kind people and wonderful food.

The recipe

— **Tim Draper, venture capital investor on the secret of success**

- ✓ Pessimists serve a purpose, but optimists accomplish.

- ✓ Work a full day and then an extra 10%. The full day is reactive, doing things people tell you to do, returning emails, checking off to-do lists. The 10% is the creative time to do proactive things—all the things that you want to do.

- ✓ The extra 10% serves the employer. It also helps you enjoy your work more. The extra 10% is what matters to you.

- ✓ Everyone's success is different.

- ✓ Look on failure as stepping stones to success.

"I missed out on Yahoo, Google and Airbnb. I missed out on Facebook. Some failures can be overcome by hard work, but failures to act are just blah."

✓ Muscles get weaker but more efficient – even the muscle between your ears.

✓ Practice the things you want to be good at, they will get easier. Fight the urge to do the same things over and over again.

✓ Try new things to live a more interesting and happy life, but expect to fail more often.

✓ Surround yourself with young, flexible minds.

✓ Love. It's very powerful.

✓ Fire people by telling them the good things about themselves. Tell them what the job required and how the two were not a fit.

✓ Respond if the media gets something wrong. Correct mistakes immediately. Errors in the press go uncontested in social media and spread geometrically.

Did you know?

- Draper is a third generation venture capitalist. Helped launch Hotmail, Skype and Tesla among others.

- His sister is actress Polly Draper of *thirtysomething*.

- A libertarian, he's behind an initiative to split California into three states.

Keep a straight face

— Annie Duke, professional poker player on the leadership lessons of Texas Hold'em

- ✓ In poker and in business look for patterns. How do opponents behave in comfortable and uncomfortable situations. Gather data so you can predict.

- ✓ Understand how opponents perceive you.

"If people are perceiving me to be too conservative, then I'll play in an incautious manner until they readjust their perception."

- ✓ Bluff sometimes in adversarial roles, but never in a partnership. People will suspect you're untrustworthy.

- ✓ Most decisions are mathematical. Take more risk when the return is huge. Take less risk when it's small. Know the pot size.

- ✓ You can't always be right. It's about being right often enough.

"Great poker players free themselves from the worry of being wrong."

- ✓ Business is not always fair. The person who does the best job doesn't always get promoted.

- ✓ It's more like poker. You can put your money in with aces and your opponent has fives. You win that pot 82% of the time, but the 18% happens.

- ✓ There are things you have control over and things that you don't. When you have a bad outcome, analyze the decision and try to figure out if you did something wrong.

"If it's out of your control, don't get tilted, which means emotionally upset. That's when we make poor decisions."

- ✓ Make decisions in your self interest, but self interest is not being overly greedy in the short run.

- ✓ Those on a good streak say, "I'm the best player in the world. Look at me, I'm so wonderful." Those on a bad streak shift blame to luck or a scapegoat. Neither attitude is helpful.

✓ Take time off when an extended bad streak affects decisions.

✓ Women are underestimated. If men think you're dumb, let them think so. Use it to your advantage

"Women spend too much time trying to prove themselves instead of saying, 'I hope everybody underestimates me.'"

✓ If you see a woman at the table, assume she's not that skilled. But the minute she puts her first chip in the pot, start updating your opinion.

✓ Smart, successful executives who try something new have to set their egos aside and say, "I'm obviously a very talented individual. I could become good at this, but I have to be willing to learn. I have to open my mind to the possibility that I'm wrong and to listen to other people." That's hard for someone who's gotten to the top.

Did you know?

- Duke was one month from defending her Ph.D. in psychology when she proposed marriage. While living in "romantic poverty" she began playing poker to pay the mortgage. Won $70,000 in her first month.

- Advanced to the finals of *Celebrity Apprentice,* where Donald Trump fired her rather than comedian Joan Rivers.

Do you believe in miracles!

— Mike Eruzione, captain of the 1980 U.S. Hockey Team on beating impossible odds

- ✓ Miracles are one part luck, nine parts hard work.

- ✓ Game winners aren't luck. They're practice and preparation unless the shot bounces off somebody's head and goes in.

- ✓ Walk out of the office every day knowing that you've given your best. It boils down to a work ethic.

"My dad told me that if I understand the value of work, at some point in life I'll be successful."

- ✓ When you fail, take all that hard work and apply it to something else.

- ✓ Peace of mind is important. If you're facing long odds, ask yourself if you have inner strength.

- ✓ A lot of dreams have long odds. Like a struggling actor, you must be happy waiting tables. If you're happy, dream on. If your miserable, move on.

41

"Don't make excuses. It's your life."

✓ Better to hire hard workers than top talent. Work with people who want to be their best. Believe in the people you work with. Do that and you win with less talent.

✓ Employees want discipline. If hockey coach Herb Brooks yelled at me I would get mad and work harder. But he never pushed us to injury.

✓ Everybody is motivated differently.

✓ "Some guys are challenged when the boss gets in their face. Others need an arm around them."

✓ Demanding leadership is most effective when used sparingly in the right situations.

✓ Hire people who are different. They may have earrings and tattoos. Great leaders change with the times, yet maintain their philosophy.

✓ Faith creates miracles. Believe in yourself. Believe in co-workers. Believe you can beat long odds.

✓ If you believe you're going to lose, you probably will.

✓ Life is miraculous even without a Miracle.

Did you know?

- Eruzione was team captain of the 1980 USA hockey team that scored the biggest upset in sports.

- The USA was seeded No. 7 and had lost to the Soviets 10-3 two weeks before. The Soviets had won 21 straight Olympic contests and had not lost gold since 1960.

- The USA tied the game at 8:39 in the last period.

- Eruzione scored the game winner 81 seconds later. It went in by a quarter inch.

"You need a bit of luck. But guess what? My shot wasn't off. It was right where I shot it."

- The story was told in the 2004 movie *Miracle* that was released months after Coach Brooks died in an auto accident.

Contemplate your navel

— Vijay Eswaran, QI Group founder on starting the day with an hour of silence

- ✓ Maintain quiet and focus for one hour. No phones, laptops, TV. If you get distracted, start again.

- ✓ Take control of where you are, where you want to go, why you need to be there.

- ✓ Still the planet, detach and take a good, hard look at yourself.

"A CEO sometimes has to be a swami sitting on a rock meditating in a lotus garden."

- ✓ The practice is called "mouna" in India – yoga of the mind. Best done two hours before the sun rises, but can be done at the end of the day. Consistency is key.

- ✓ The point is to go deeper.

- ✓ First, analyze yesterday. Note progress and identify reasons for failure. Derive lessons.

✓ Second, plan goals for today, tomorrow, next week.

✓ Third, plan long-term goals. List what you plan to achieve in a year and beyond. Do long-term planning every time.

✓ Chinese saying: "A beggar lives meal to meal. A peasant lives day to day. A farmer lives season to season. A nobleman lives year to year. A king lives 10 years at a time, but an emperor lives a century at a time."

✓ Fourth, think on challenges. What you are dealing with. What should you do? Let answers materialize.

"It's a time of asking questions as you would to a buddy, looking upon your Maker as a guide."

✓ Fifth, seek knowledge by reading a non-fiction book or listening to an educational CD for 10 minutes. Summarize what is learned.

✓ Detachment does not mean dispassion or apathy. It's the reverse. It's the ability to love more deeply, to care, to feel more deeply. One can only do that when not attached to emotions. Emotions get in the way, particularly when they involve the people we love.

✓ A CEO has souls that are dependent upon him. That makes detachment more vital.

"Stop letting life pick you up like a piece of driftwood, and throw you back to shore every once in a while."

✓ Sixth, commune with the Lord for the last 10 minutes. Ask questions in your heart that need answers. Write it down.

✓ Walk into meetings with a new armory of information that looks like it's coming off the cuff. Mouna is like an athlete or pianist practicing mentally before they play. It will make you mentally fit, faster on the uptake.

✓ An hour of silence is like exercise. A person who never does it would rather get shot than get started. Once started, he would rather die than stop.

Did you know?

- Eswaran is a Malaysian citizen of Indian origin.

- Receives standing ovations from Indian businessmen after speeches that declare "this is India's millennium."

- Took an oath of silence for 33 days after graduating college.

- QI Group is an Asian conglomerate that employs 1,500 people in 30 countries.

Running with the big boys

— John Fisher, Saucony CEO 1991-2005 on being David vs. a Goliath named Nike

- ✓ Feel like a minnow next to a whale? Do what Dr Pepper does against Coke. Create charisma, ask for loyalty.

- ✓ Build dealer relationships. Nike can run a $50 million ad campaign, but Saucony has clinics on Tuesdays for the Happy Valley Roadrunners Club. Accompany customers on weekly runs, do grass-roots and guerrilla marketing. Grow organically.

- ✓ Find a niche where you compete against players your own size. Customer loyalty is easier to obtain inside a small niche.

"Loyalty is key. If you have it, big companies can run ads until they're blue in the face."

- ✓ Stick with your niche. Don't make a Dr Pepper cola or Dr Pepper ginger ale.

✓ Cheer the success of giant companies. Welcome their advertising. The stronger they are, the healthier the industry.

✓ Hire away smart minds who want less bureaucracy and the opportunity to make an impact.

✓ Take advantage of being nimble and less bureaucratic. Small companies seldom start trends, but they can react and get to market.

✓ With every decision, step back and say, "Is this a best practice, or is there a better way to do it?"

✓ Fly under the radar. Small companies make controversial decisions, such as moving production from Maine to China, without as much negative fallout.

Did you know?

- Fisher taught economics at Chamberlayne Junior College before joining Saucony in 1973.

- Ran the 100th Boston Marathon in 1996. Time: 4 hours, 30 minutes.

- Passion is racing grand prix sailboats. Winner of several major East Coast yachting regattas.

When good people say goodbye

— Eric Foss, Pepsi Bottling CEO 2006-10 on retaining talent

- ✓ People quit when they feel under-appreciated. Give your best employees stretch assignments, profit-and-loss responsibility. Raises are often less important than career opportunities.

- ✓ A single departure is not worrisome, but watch for patterns.

- ✓ Exiting employees blame ineffective managers. Great bosses are the accelerator of high-potential employees. Bad bosses are the biggest decelerator.

- ✓ Leadership is about coaching a teachable point of view.

- ✓ It's a myth that all fresh ideas come from new hires. On the other hand, longevity isn't the same as success. Retain talent, but develop fresh talent as well. Ask: Is this somebody with high growth potential, who can make a long-term contribution?

50

✓ No system compensates for a bad hire. Exercise patience. Look for character. Make sure the team will have a shared set of characteristics: courage, the willingness to take risks, confidence.

✓ Invest in employee development. Some will take their training to other companies. Employee pirating frustrates, but it's the price you pay.

✓ Learn from exit interviews. If those leaving say they felt under-appreciated, a culture of recognition needs to be a part of the company DNA.

✓ Forget about those who leave. Wake up caring about the people who stay.

✓ Let meetings be contentious and respectful. Intervene if the line is crossed. Encourage people to have a point of view, and make sure they feel comfortable expressing it.

"If everyone's thinking alike, then someone's not thinking."

✓ Raise the bar. Provide no place to hide and lethargic employees will self-select out.

Did you know?

- Foss has a 15 golf handicap and coached the basketball teams of his three daughters when they were young.

- Now CEO of Aramark, a food, facilities and uniform services company.

God herds cats

— **Israel Gaither, Salvation Army National Commander 2006-10 on a sense of mission**

✓ Begin the day with worship. Make commitments and live them. Don't exist for yourself, exist to give yourself away.

✓ Ask God to protect you, your mind, your thinking, your behavior.

✓ Nobody's perfect. Remind yourself of that and watch for your flaws, not the weaknesses of others.

"I'm not here to judge. I believe that the way to the best leadership is modeling Jesus."

✓ God uses the gifts and efforts of business. People like Joan Kroc, Bill Gates and others are part of the capitalistic nature of America and are giving. Fight the slide into materialism and secularism. Return to root, spiritual values. Salute and humbly thank those doing their part.

✓ Are you at the right company? The question to ask is: Do I believe in the value and integrity of the product or service?

✓ Ask: Is this mission worthy? Test new ideas against the mission purpose.

✓ There's always a tug on leaders. Everyone needs a piece of you. Everyone wants your company to be something different. Be courageous enough to say "that's really not what we do."

✓ No job is more insignificant than others. The person who cleans the bathrooms is keeping it attractive so others will feel comfortable.

✓ When a worker's not performing, go alongside, pick up, teach and engage. But those who don't keep up with the standards, practices and policies, they shouldn't be in that job. Fire them compassionately, with a firm understanding of what's expected.

Did you know?

- Gaither is known for his singing voice.

- He was the Salvation Army's first African-American national commander. Married to Eva Gaither, a fifth-generation Salvationist. First racially integrated marriage of U.S. Salvation Army officers

- Peter Drucker called the Salvation Army the most effective organization, coordinating 3,700 officers, 113,000 soldiers, 423,000 members, 61,000 employees and 3.5 million volunteers.

Capitalism vs. Socialism

— Stuart Graham, Skanska CEO 2002-08 on Sweden's pros and cons

✓ For good or bad, nations gravitate toward socialism. Europe is the oldest of Western economies and citizens look for more leisure time and support from the government. Even China will trend toward Europe's philosophy eventually.

✓ The key is to find a way to prosper. Sweden is technologically connected. It takes a long-term perspective. There is less incentive to distribute earnings and dividends, so companies invest in the future of the business. Investment pays off in productivity and performance.

✓ Healthcare is a mess everywhere. Many Americans are uninsured. In Europe, they have universal healthcare, but patients are inconvenienced and their care severely restricted.

"Waiting six months for surgery is terrible. Who knows what country has the best healthcare system."

✓ In all countries, big business has a bad image to the man on the street. It's counter-intuitive, but the corporate tax rate is lower and the individual tax rate is much higher in Sweden than in the U.S.

✓ The global economy grows ever intense. There will be no letup in the demands for financial performance. There will be no letup in the demands for social programs. Management is under pressure to get better.

✓ Sweden's Social Democrats were defeated in 2006 for the second time in 70 years because adjustments were needed for a stronger economy.

✓ CEOs everywhere are criticized for being overpaid, even in Sweden where they are paid much less.

✓ Productivity isn't country-specific. Workers are willing and unwilling everywhere. Supervision is key.

✓ Diversity is important, but quotas should be avoided. In Norway, 40% of directors must be women.

✓ Don't travel to another country and tell everyone that Americans have the answers.

"Even if you go from New York to West Virginia, it's not a good idea to tell everybody how smart you are and how dumb they are."

✓ The U.S. is envied for economic prowess and success. As long as it's on top, it will be unpopular for its foreign policies and politics.

✓ The greatest opportunity remains in America. Immigrants prosper here.

Did you know?

• Graham, an American, ran the Swedish construction giant based in Stockholm. If Skanska were a U.S. company, it would have been ranked No. 125 on the Fortune 500.

• Favorite Swedish dish: Salmon. Favorite music group: Not Abba.

Mopping up the mess

— Jamie Houghton, Corning CEO 1983-96; 2002-05 on returning as a boomerang leader

- ✓ Boomerang CEOs are appropriate when circumstances are dire. Good succession planning is preferable, but a boomerang CEO is better than an outsider.

- ✓ Expect to find things done differently when you come back.

- ✓ At 68, don't expect to have the energy of a 47-year-old. Slow down. No 50 trips a year. Let the board know you'll take a measured pace.

- ✓ The longer you've been absent, the greater the challenge. Court the advice of rising leaders.

- ✓ Stay as long as necessary, but not too long. Don't announce your departure in advance, or everybody will be looking to the next team. Don't be a lame duck.

"My druthers is to turn the company over to new eyes and ears."

✓ Watch your ego. When you leave for good, the lights don't go out.

✓ Don't boomerang twice. The third time is not charm.

Did you know?

- Houghton's the great-great-grandson of the company founder. He was brought back when Corning stock fell from $113 to $1 a share.

- There have been many other boomerang CEOs including Harry Stonecipher at Boeing, Henry Schacht at Lucent.

- Collects suspenders from around the world. Avid fisherman. Fan of opera and chamber music. Favorite opera: Don Giovanni.

- Walks several miles a day with a cane after stepping in front of a car in 1993.

Taking business to school

— Molly Howard, 2008 school principal of the year on leadership lessons from the world of public education

- ✓ Know where you're going before you lead.

- ✓ Have passion, high expectations, and a can-do attitude.

- ✓ So what if you're a school superintendent or CEO. There's little power in a title or position. Power emanates from relationships.

- ✓ Business has an advantage and should retain the ability to fire bad employees and reward good ones with pay raises.

"Education is a zero-reject business. Companies can pick and choose raw materials. That's a big, big difference."

- ✓ Don't give up on certain employees. Students that succeed in life are usually future-oriented and goal-focused. However, slow-starters can be wildly successful. Valedictorians sometimes drop out of college.

✓ Revisit Stephen Covey's "Seek First to Understand, Then to be Understood" (Habit 5 of *The 7 Habits of Highly Effective People*). When someone complains, leaders don't have to agree, but they must understand.

✓ Inspect what you expect. Use standards and accountability. Don't be Big Brother watching, but look at the data to make sure it's happening.

"Teachers don't get to spend the entire semester on World War II because they'd like to."

✓ The best road to performance is buy-in. It's all William Edwards Deming stuff. Be familiar with total quality management. Buy-in is more powerful than the directives that leaders send down.

✓ Teachers must see themselves as empowered leaders. Everyone is a teacher-leader.

✓ Model hard work.

✓ Be visible at extracurricular events.

✓ You don't have control over the private lives of your workers. You have control over your beliefs. Believe that all can learn to high levels.

✓ Sometimes it's not what is implemented, but what you stop doing. Good schools eliminate dual-track, where children take a watered-down curriculum.

✓ When an assignment is turned in that doesn't meet or exceed the standard, the teacher says, "Do this again. This is not acceptable work." Don't give zeros. The power of zero is astronomical. It destroys motivation. Just don't accept less than what people are capable of doing.

✓ Likewise, there is no room for a marginal teacher. Build a scaffold for employees to reach the highest mark.

"If you just raise the bar it doesn't mean people are going to jump higher."

✓ A glut of information can make a school or company data-rich and information-poor. Ask the right question, and then turn to the data for the answer.

Don't look at the numbers and ask what do they mean?

Did you know?

- Howard was principal of Jefferson County High in small-town Louisville, Ga. where 80% of students live in poverty. Eliminated remedial courses.

- Kept the phone numbers of habitually late or absent students on her bedroom mirror and phoned them in the morning. She sometimes went to their homes to get them out of bed to take tests.

- Recommends that business leaders read books by education guru Michael Fullan.

- She's now superintendent.

Innovate or die

— Jeffrey Immelt, General Electric CEO 2000-17 on R&D spending in a slow economy

✓ Talk to your sales force. They'll tell you that it's easier to sell great products.

✓ The way to grow is through innovation.

"It's not just a nice-to-do, but a real priority."

✓ Great technology is the way to protect profit margins.

✓ Get customer inputs early on to introduce complex technologies faster and with higher quality.

✓ Know how to hit singles. Home runs like hydrogen fuel cells, molecular imaging and nanotechnology take a long time. Introduce technologies with a variety of cycle times. Work on the next generation and implement the current generation at the same time.

"Get out of balance and get broken."

✓ Expect failures.

✓ Move some R&D offshore to get broad exposure to ideas, to talent, to growth and to markets. Utilize every global brain you can find.

✓ Don't try to grow a company outside the U.S. and have all of your products designed inside.

Did you know?

- Immelt earned a degree in applied mathematics at Dartmouth, where he played football. Harvard MBA.

- Jack Welch hand-picked him from a stable of contenders, including James McNerney (who became CEO at 3M and Boeing) and Robert Nardelli (Home Depot and Chrysler).

- Immelt's father worked at GE for 38 years.

- GE under-performed and in 2018 became the last of the original 19th-century companies to be dropped from the Dow Jones Industrial Average.

The ugly American

— **Kazuo Inamori, Kyocera founder on anti-U.S. sentiment**

✓ Foreigners dislike the USA because it is dominant militarily. America is feared.

✓ The stronger America and its companies become, the more humble they must be.

✓ Anti-American sentiment doesn't come from Islam. It stems from poverty, not religion.

✓ U.S. business leaders should help people in other parts of the world – for the sake of humanity.

"Humble behavior is required."

✓ U.S. leaders are skilled. They are creative and ingenious in finding new ways to run a business. They are dedicated, both physically and spiritually, to the management of their companies.

✓ Pay for performance is good, executive greed is not.

✓ CEO pay tempts character. If U.S executive compensation were lower, more scandals would be avoided. Share corporate profits with directors, officers, general managers, department heads and tens of thousands of other employees.

✓ When a performance-based compensation system boosts motivation to work harder, it is a good system.

"In the past, the Japanese were hard-working. In my opinion, U.S. leaders now work harder."

✓ Spend 30 minutes to one hour each day reading philosophy or religion. Walk in a righteous direction.

✓ Talents can drive away wonderful personalities. The proverb, "A genius drowns in his talents," warns of that. Talent needs to be exercised with character and integrity.

Did you know?

- Inamori was born to a poor family in Kagoshima City, Japan. Founded Kyoto Ceramic in 1959. Founded DDI, Japan's second-largest telecommunications company, in 1984.

- At 77, he became CEO of Japan Airlines when it entered bankruptcy protection. Led it to re-listing on the Tokyo Stock Exchange.

- Entered Buddhist priesthood in 1997 at the Enpuku-ji temple in Kyoto. Received Buddhist name Daiwa, meaning Big Harmony.

Target the audience

— Tom Joyner, radio host on the African-American market

- ✓ African-Americans spend $1.2 trillion a year. Capture it.

- ✓ Don't try to catch African-American consumers with a broad net. Target them unashamedly.

- ✓ *Ebony* magazine convinced advertisers to use black models in print ads 50 years ago. Generations remain loyal to those brands.

- ✓ Southwest Airlines recognized Black History Month at their gates. Royal Caribbean sponsored cruises. Upscale African-Americans respond to targeted advertising.

- ✓ Car dealerships have radio ads enticing African-Americans with bad credit. That doesn't offend them because they believe they've been discriminated against by zip code.

"We face redlining and profiling. You need a car and you ain't got no credit. Waive the credit check. No one else will."

✓ Commercials that portray black women as sassy and black men greet each other with "Whassup?" are not offensive. They are not the modern-day equivalent of Aunt Jemima and Uncle Ben. McDonald's didn't cross a line when they had African-Americans say, "I'd hit it," which suggested in hip-hop slang that they'd make love to a double cheeseburger.

"Pop culture is not the same as Hambone and 'Yessir, boss, try my biscuits.'"

✓ Target the Hispanic market similarly.

Did you know?

- Joyner is a vegetarian. Keeps his age a secret.

- Father was a Tuskegee Airman.

- Earned the nickname "The Fly Jock" when he flew between a morning job in Dallas and an afternoon job in Chicago from 1986 to 1993.

"A celebrity is somebody who sleeps late. I'm well known, but I get up too early to be a celebrity."

71

Hit me

— Bill Kaplan, blackjack card counter on applying 21 to everyday business

- ✓ Seek opportunity and disequilibrium in the marketplace. Manage and mitigate risk, generate long-run returns without being beat by short-term swings.

- ✓ Pool capital and people. Little can be done with one person and a small amount of money.

- ✓ Change strategies as conditions evolve.

"We hit casinos when they first opened, when they were still figuring out how to run things."

- ✓ Tech companies burnt through millions and went broke, even though they had a business model that worked. If you bet $500,000 a hand, even with a 1% advantage, you get wiped out if you lose one or two hands in the short run. The variance killed dot-com companies.

✓ Understand things from the investors' perspective. Give players a significant stake in the outcome.

✓ Unnecessary risk was taken in the subprime mortgage debacle because they were playing with someone else's money.

✓ If it's a cash business, run revenue through a simulation to see if it's within one or two standard deviations. That exposes thieves. Hire the right people, train them, motivate them, provide incentives.

✓ Build a team culture.

Did you know?

- Kaplan trained more than 100 students in card counting and won $10 million over 15 years as coach of the MIT Blackjack Team.

- Made famous by the 2008 movie *21* starring Kevin Spacey.

- Gave up blackjack for real estate.

Leadership is exhausting

— Ewald Kist, ING CEO 2000-04 on the importance of physical fitness

✓ Trim executives run trim companies.

✓ The business world requires endurance. Get physically fit to be mentally fit.

✓ Sports do something to you, especially team sports and extreme sports.

"Sports taught me to do the extra mile."

✓ Too busy? Leaders know how to plan, so make time. Make exercise an addiction.

✓ Don't carry a phone when exercising. You won't miss anything important.

✓ Nudge others at your company to get fit.

"If I see someone who is too fat, I will say something. People know, but they need a little pressure."

- ✓ Exercise in solitude to problem solve. Think about complicated issues.

- ✓ Eat fruit.

- ✓ Work hard, but don't be a workaholic. Come to work refreshed on Monday.

- ✓ Run in the evening to refresh your mind.

"I live on the beach in The Hague in Holland. They have fantastic dunes that I run."

- ✓ Expect to slow down with age, but don't stop.

- ✓ Run when traveling. Run worldwide. Every culture's accustomed to seeing runners.

Did you know?

- Kist played for Holland on the 1968 Olympic field hockey team.

- Took up marathon running at age 45. Skated in the 11-Cities Tour, a 124-mile, all-day skating race over lakes and canals in Holland.

- His father was a Supreme Court judge in the Netherlands.

Should we lead like George Patton or Mr. Rogers?

— A.G. Lafley, Procter & Gamble CEO 2000-10 on being an effective boss

- ✓ Self-sacrifice is huge. You can't do the job unless you're willing to put the greater good first. You pay for it in your personal life, in your family life. Some people pay for it in their health. Put the company and others ahead of personal aspirations.

- ✓ Be demanding of others, but don't be mean-spirited. Use language less colorful than Patton's. Don't carry a riding whip.

"I'm not wearing my cardigan sweater today, but I certainly would never be confused with Patton."

- ✓ Be like King Henry V in Shakespeare. He stayed up all night and walked and talked with his troops before they went into action the next day. Care about people, even those who fail.

✓ By all means, manage by walking around – but be on time for meetings.

✓ Hold people accountable. If they fall way short, it can be the end of their career at your company. They have to decide what they're going to do next.

"All failure is learning."

✓ Mistakes – yours and others – should come early, fast and cheap, not after billions of dollars are invested.

✓ Lead with your head and your heart. If you lead with heart only, you'll make bad decisions because emotions will fool you. If you lead with head only, you may be abandoned by your team in really tough circumstances.

✓ CEOs make two kinds of decisions. (1) Big decisions that aren't difficult. They are blazingly clear. (2) Decisions that have no good solution. They are dilemmas and can't be solved. These must be managed.

✓ What separates talented people is the courage to make the really hard call. Some calls are tough because they are hard to figure out. Others are tough because they entail short-term sacrifice.

✓ It's human nature to avoid hard decisions. Leaders buck human nature.

✓ Some of the strongest, most courageous people are on the minority side of a decision. Listen to those who have the courage to speak.

✓ At meetings, before listening to solutions, make sure everyone has a clear definition of the problem. Hold off on advocacy until all possible solutions are on the table. Sort through the options. Then, and only then, let people advocate.

✓ People who rise have uncompromising integrity both in the moral sense, and in the sense of thinking with integrity and acting with integrity.

✓ The best think with discipline and honesty. They come to grips with reality, and bring incredible integrity to the decision and the action.

"Sort through flattery, through politics, and see things as they are."

✓ Some decisions take a minute, some weeks or months. Avoid the tendency to create crises that don't exist.

✓ If you're highly compensated be generous. Don't be ostentatious. No yachts. No trophy cars. Be boring, like Mr. Rogers.

✓ Leaders aren't born, they are clearly made. Choose to lead. Choose to make a difference, to make the world better in some meaningful way. Until that choice is made, you are a lump of clay.

Did you know?

• Lafley collects baseball cards, comic books and rock 'n' roll vinyl records.

• Named one of America's Best Leaders by Harvard's Kennedy School of Government.

Take a stand or get run over

— Edward Liddy, Allstate CEO 1999-2008 on lobbying congress

- ✓ Formulate a point of view that's good for your company, your customers.

- ✓ Work with Democrats and Republicans.

- ✓ Public stands cause controversy, but you can't always be neutral. Choose positions carefully, but be politically active to advance certain things.

- ✓ The risk of boycotts and other backlash is often less than the risk of doing nothing. Don't put the banner in your hands and lead the charge, but sometimes you have to take a side.

- ✓ Don't fear lawsuits. Rely on the ballot box – and the jury box.

- ✓ The meter is pretty expensive when it's running on lawsuits. Settle sometimes. Other times, settlements will give rise to a thousand more suits. In that case litigate. Don't be known by lawyers as a soft company.

✓ Regulation is not free. Side airbags save lives, but consumers may not want to pay for it. Make some cars with side airbags, some without. Educate the public, let it know the risk. Then, let consumers decide.

✓ Pressure Congress to limit punitive damages. It's better to remove a bad doctor than to drive up insurance bills that are passed on to consumers.

✓ Seal evidence in a settled lawsuit, not to cover up a harmful product, but because the company never had a chance at rebuttal. Don't seal to hide things, but to keep untruths from going public.

"It's like a divorce proceeding. Anyone can say anything they want in a lawsuit, whether it's grounded in fact or not."

✓ There will always be frivolous lawsuits in America. It's cultural.

✓ The public has a reason to mistrust big organizations. WorldCom and Enron cost people billions of dollars.

81

✓ Do your job right. Bring about a more wholesome view of business. The American capitalist system is the envy of and the engine of growth around the world. Keep it that way.

"I have a son in college. If he tells people that his dad is the CEO of Allstate, they look at him like he's some sort of crook."

Did you know?

- Liddy chaired the Business Roundtable's Civil Justice Reform Task Force that lobbied for a 2005 law that sent most class-action lawsuits into federal courts. It was regarded as a victory for business, as was a bankruptcy bill that made it more difficult for consumers to avoid paying debt.

Cleaning up the mess

— Peter Löscher, Siemens CEO 2007-13 on taking over an unethical company accused of bribery

✓ Decisions to act unethically and illegally destroy the lives of thousands of honest, hard-working employees. Many fall hard when leaders abdicate their responsibility.

✓ New leadership must make things right in the shortest time possible.

✓ Fire former executives. Bring in your own team.

✓ Stick to principles. Be a trusted role model with absolute clarity.

"Anyone who has ever sailed knows that there is only one true north."

✓ Win in the marketplace, not by cheating, but by out-innovating competitors.

✓ True leaders have a set of core values they commit to and live by in good times and bad.

✓ True leaders don't go with the tide.

"Beware of the phrase: 'Don't worry, we can get away with it because everybody does.' The most dangerous words in business are, 'Everybody does it.'"

✓ Different countries abide by different rules. But ethics apply universally. In Spain, the U.S., Japan and Germany, the most successful businesses are the most ethical.

✓ Never waste a good crisis. Bad times give license for wholesale change. Use it to transform the company. Change the culture.

✓ Be born into a family with ethical parents guided by a moral compass. Stress the values of hard work, fairness, trust and a sense of belonging.

✓ There is no conflict between success and ethics. The only guarantee for a good life is to live as a good person.

Did you know?

- Löscher was hired as CEO of Siemens to clean up a global scandal that cost the company a record $1.34 billion in fines for paying bribes and kickbacks to secure contracts worldwide.

- Graduated from Gymnasium Villach, Austria in 1978; master's degree at the Vienna University of Economics and Business Administration. Attended MBA program at the Chinese University of Hong Kong. Speaks German, English, French, Spanish, and Japanese.

When you're let go at 39

— Ronnie Lott, NFL Hall-of-Famer on making life's transitions

- ✓ Retiring athletes ask: "What can I do? What should I do?" The hard part is stepping into the unknown of a new game.

- ✓ It's the same with everyone making a transition. Challenges can be overwhelming and can cripple. Move forward. Know that you have to invest a lot of energy and time to achieve.

- ✓ Don't let insecurity keep you sidelined. Maybe you'll get belittled for being dumb. Get over those fears. That's very difficult to execute, but do it anyway.

  "You have to know you're going to fumble."

- ✓ Swallow your pride. Bring the right energy, the right ch'i, the right moxie to attain greatness.

- ✓ Become a rookie again. Learn the nuances, a new playbook. People fail when they take shortcuts.

✓ You're as good as your new skills and the perfection of those skills.

"When you're a rookie, you're a number. You don't even have a name."

✓ Listen to smart people in the new arena. Be around people you admire.

✓ Know there is more to you. You might not get the feedback. Self-examine and self-reflect as much as possible.

"It's like players who invest time looking at film. Reflect on things you want to achieve each day."

✓ Maybe you're not a first-rounder in business. The fifth- and sixth-rounders end up making a huge difference.

✓ There are those who might not have the best resume but have the right attributes to make others better who are around them.

✓ Tap into the competitive spirit. It takes spirit to dive into a new manual on how to sell software.

- ✓ Save when you're making money. Preserve capital. Think like the Rockefellers and leave a legacy.

- ✓ Use your brand as equity to leverage your ability to bring eyeballs or relationships. A lot of life is about opening doors.

- ✓ Harris Barton was not famous and he knew football was not going to last forever. He took stationery from his team and wrote letters to local executives and invited them to lunch. He has the Rolodex of a Steve Young or a Joe Montana. He wanted to have success after he was through playing and assimilate himself into society.

Did you know?

- Lott played 14 NFL seasons (1981-94), 10 with the San Francisco 49ers, who won eight division titles and four Super Bowls. Elected to Pro Football Hall of Fame.

- Had the tip of his injured finger amputated in 1985 to avoid missing games.

Real teammates pull 'til they puke

— Dan Lyons, Olympic rower on the leadership lessons of an oarsman

✓ Ancient Greek Olympians competed to win. There was no silver medal. They also competed within the rules. Referees flogged wrestlers if they tried to gouge someone's eye. Strive for the ideal. Lend nobility to the effort.

✓ Business is a team sport. Leaders gain command of the power of everybody in the boat.

✓ The stroke sits in the stern, looking backward. He sets the rhythm. He can't see the rest of the crew, but the crew can see the stroke. He has a great sense of self, rhythm and consistency.

✓ Without leadership consistency, the team can't get into a flow. That's why Wall Street is concerned about changes in leadership.

✓ Each time a rower puts the oar in the water he leaves a puddle, a tangible reminder of his presence. That puddle has a look and feel to it. The stroke-leader sees those puddles – and knows.

✓ Leaders use their senses and attune themselves. They feel who is early and who is late. They feel subtle changes.

✓ The race is 2,000 meters. Crews will be in it for the first half. But an experienced eye will see the strain. Some team members want to pull really hard at the beginning, others at the end. The leader's job is to get everyone to apply power at the same time.

✓ Leaders exponentially magnify the team's power. The strain becomes easier.

✓ Leaders communicate in every way, even with eye contact and energy. It's not just what they say, but how it's said.

✓ Be positive, not curt or abrupt. How do you affect the room – or boat? Bring a positive surge of power, not a negative surge that breeds frustration or anger.

✓ High-performance teams are like cults. They're on a mission. That's what appealing to the spirit is all about. Everyone on the team has an enormous fear of letting the group down.

✓ Everyone wants to be valued and a part of something bigger.

"Throughout military history, people have gone willingly into situations where they are apt to be killed. In sports and business, lives aren't on the line. But team bonds are established."

✓ In business, sports and politics, getting everyone to apply power evenly is about controlling egos. There's always dynamic tension between R&D, sales and production because they make different promises to different people. Leadership is getting them to sublimate their own agendas for the company's agenda.

✓ A leader paints a vision of what is possible and reaches down into your psyche and says, "This is your destiny."

✓ You can ennoble garbage collection if you let people know it's important. It's as simple as that.

"Everyone wants to be a part of something bigger."

✓ There are people who make a boat go, when on paper, they shouldn't. There is a practice in rowing called "seat racing." You run two boats side by side for five minutes. Then you switch the bowmen. You go mano a mano with the two bowmen because all else is equal.

✓ Managers can use the equivalent of seat racing in business. Put a new person on a team to see if group dynamics change. It's chemistry. The person swapped out may perform better in another group.

"I've coached kids who, on paper, are 10 seconds slower, but somehow move the boat. I call them the glue men, the bonding agents."

✓ The best team members feed off each other. They are a little quirky and odd. Bland groups, no matter how strong and powerful, underperform. That's the strength of diversity. It's not just racial or ethnic or gender diversity, it's diversity of spirit, of seeing life and the world.

✓ Rowing rewards focus. There are so many variables: the wind, the current, uncustomary noise. The natural world impinges externally. Internally, eight people try to move as one. The successful focus entirely on the moment, making minute adjustments.

✓ Anything can happen, and it usually does. A little wake can knock the boat. Teams adjust instantaneously and think, "Wow, this is so cool."

✓ As soon as you start to look behind you at what just happened, or look ahead too far, you're in trouble. You have a grand plan, but at any moment you have to be absolutely focused on what's going on.

✓ Be consistent. Don't be happy one day and moody and angry the next. If a coxswain changes from 30 to 29 strokes a minute on a whim, the crew can fall apart and take several strokes to readjust to the new rhythm.

Did you know?

- Lyons is president of leadership consultants Team Concepts. He's a graduate of the U.S. Naval Academy. He rowed on seven U.S. National Teams, winning two world bronze medals, a world gold and a Pan American gold. Member of U.S. Rowing Hall of Fame.

- Competed in the 1988 Seoul Olympics in the coxed pair. Was among the favorites to win before partner Robert Espeseth came down sick. Finished 11th.

- Best known in rowing quarters for being a part of the 1986 Mutiny at Oxford when Americans boycotted the annual race vs. Cambridge in a protest over favoritism in the selection of crew members.

Wave the magic wand

— Lorin Maazel, Music Director New York Philharmonic 2002-09 on leading like a conductor

✓ A conductor is the musical equivalent of a stage director. Actors know their parts, but the director is responsible for the overall picture.

✓ Each musician knows the best way to do the job. The conductor brings musician A and musician B together.

✓ Players battle with their instruments. Know that they want to do their best.

✓ Don't frown and complain.

✓ Musical notes on a page are lifeless. Push each instrument to achieve a goal. Know the score and understand the problems the players will encounter playing it.

"No conductor accomplishes anything without commanding respect of the players."

✓ Don't ask for respect. It will be accorded to leaders who know their job, know the business, know the people, and show respect for them.

✓ In rehearsal, conductors mess up by stopping to say something. But then the music sounds exactly as it did before. Never say anything that's not going to make a difference.

"Don't stop the orchestra just to hear yourself talk."

Envy is the wind that fills the sails of human affairs. Those who are in leadership can expect unjust treatment.

✓ Don't curry favor. Leaders don't last long when they take the boys out and get drunk at the local pub. If you're affectionate and have friendly feelings toward people, you will win their affection.

✓ Leaders are both born and made. You're born potentially a great conductor, but then comes the discipline. Years and years of study, focus and stick-to-it-tiveness to the point where you can't study another note.

✓ All the studying in the world does not make you a conductor. I've seen people eminently prepared, and they don't have the natural gift. That's true of everything – playing chess, tennis. There are actors who walk onto the theater stage with a commanding presence. Others scream and tear their hair, and the audience yawns. Some folks have natural authority. It can't be defined. They've just got it.

✓ There is more similarity between oboe players from opposite ends of the earth than there is between people of the same country. A Japanese oboe player is more like a French oboe player than he would be to a sumo wrestler.

✓ If everyone seems tired, it's you. It's projection. Players are as sluggish as the conductor. Come to work fresh, energetic, projecting enthusiasm and go-go-go. Be irresistible. If you're not up to it, take a cold shower. It's your job to energize people.

"Music making without emotion and passion is nothing."

✓ Take responsibility for failure, even when it has nothing to do with you. It relaxes followers.

✓ Losing your temper is a non-starter. Fine orchestras respect themselves and have a great sense of mission and *esprit de corps* . They're trying to do their best.

"Don't look for a perfect performance. Look for an impassioned performance."

✓ To be a good leader, first learn to be a good follower. Sit in the orchestra and learn how depressing it is to follow someone you cannot respect either professionally or personally.

✓ When you're young, you're arrogant. Learn to be humble and have self-confidence. Some performers are self-destructive. They don't do their best because they're always tearing their performances apart, always feeling inadequate. Others are totally in love with themselves, incredibly arrogant. Find the balance between self-confidence and humility.

✓ Ask people to stretch. Push and pull them. Look out and say, "Yes, you can." It's like the childhood ditty about the little engine that could. Bring people past the limitations of their own potential. That's leadership. All fine conductors have it.

Did you know?

- Maazel has a photographic memory.

- First violin lesson at age 5; conducting lesson at 7; conducted the Interlochen Orchestra at the 1939 New York World's Fair at 9. Conducted most major U.S. orchestras between ages 9 and 15.

- Best-selling album: *Sentimento.*

Reading the tea leaves

— Frank MacInnis, Emcor Group CEO 1994-2011 on emerging from Chapter 11 in an unpredictable economy

✓ When workers are terminated, persuade those left behind to believe in themselves and to work as hard as possible. Instill a message of hope and pride among the damaged.

✓ Consider keeping executives who weathered a realistic storm. Dump those who had an appetite for debt and grandiose visions that failed.

✓ Know who your friends are. Not everyone is against you. Friends can be customers, vendors, union relationships. They'll make concessions if they know that they will be a part of your future.

✓ The guardianship of capital is the primary responsibility. Let go of assets that you'd love to keep in other circumstances, but just can't afford.

- ✓ Hurry. The sooner you get out of bankruptcy, the better the chance of survival. The Chapter 11 stigma gets heavier. People get dispirited. Money owed to you is a declining asset because some will hold back payments to see if compromises are available.

"A prompt decision, even if wrong, is better than a late decision."

- ✓ Assess the strength of the economy. If your sector is adding people, it is making a serious and expensive bet on the future.

- ✓ Learn from customers. If they make decisions that involve large capital deployment, conclude that they must be counting on profitability. Watch for defensive moves in anticipation of sector downturns.

- ✓ Business is made up of optimistic people, some to a fault. Curb enthusiasm and understand that there are dispassionate economic forces at work. Watch for the next recession, look for evidence every day. It's coming.

- ✓ If the whole industry is troubled, the likelihood of your company succeeding post-bankruptcy is better.

It's hard to battle companies that are prosperous and capital rich and ready to beat your brains out.

✓ If customers lengthen payment periods, they are concerned about liquidity. This is a useful guide to impending recession even before people talk about it formally.

"There's no sterner test than keeping the lid on disaster."

✓ Nothing's more frustrating than to be tapped out at the bank and have something astonishingly good come to your attention. When you have no debt you'll hear from bankers and companies with assets to sell of high quality at reasonable prices.

✓ A strong balance sheet poorly managed will get a worse credit rating than a weak balance sheet in the hands of principled, disciplined management.

✓ Read as much as possible about broad trends.

"Think in the bathtub like Alan Greenspan. Wherever your do you best thinking is where you ought to be."

✓ Every CEO decides how to allocate capital between risk and reward. Once you're back on your feet, take

102

some risk. But never again put all your assets into a perceived trend.

✓ It's nice to agree with smart people, but you can't always follow the herd mentality. It's often wrong. Think for yourself.

Did you know?

- MacInnis took over Emcor in 2002 when it was in Chapter 11. Five years later the stock was up 1,360 percent. He missed predicting the Great Recession of 2008.

- Began construction career in Tehran, Iran. Worked in Baghdad, Bangkok, the United Arab Emirates, London and Oklahoma. Retired to Westport, Conn.

Deal or no deal

— **Howie Mandel, TV game show host on the awful risk of getting caught up in the emotion of the moment**

- ✓ The game show *Deal or No Deal* was a study in human nature. A scary number of contestants were comfortable leaving with nothing. They'd forfeit $250,000 for the chance at $1 million.

- ✓ $50,000 is a down payment on a home. It's a life-changing amount. Don't be a moron. Take the money and go home. Put your kids through college.

  "It's not fear vs. greed. It's fear vs. dreams."

- ✓ Don't be a coulda, shoulda, woulda person. Be content.

- ✓ Contrary to beliefs, women take more risk. They were the biggest winners – and losers – on the show.

- ✓ Most contestants started with a game plan. They said, "If I get a $100,000 offer, I'm going home." But then they got emotionally involved by the lights, the crowd, the atmosphere.

"One lady's dream was $75,000 to open a pastry shop. She turned down $78,000. The offer fell to $30,000, but she played on and it went back to $76,000. Opportunity knocked twice. She went home with $5."

✓ Think worst-case. There is nobility in being risk averse.

Did you know?

- Mandel says he's risk averse, but he owned a carpet company in Canada and was making six figures. He gave it up to make $9,000 his first year as a comedian.

- Expelled from high school for a practical joke. He told a construction company that he was on the school board and ordered an addition to the school.

- Color-blind. Germ-phobic. Won't shake hands.

- Played Dr. Wayne Fiscus on TV show *St. Elsewhere*. Creator and producer of children's series *Bobby's World*, which ran eight seasons and is syndicated in 65 countries.

- *Deal or No Deal* was based on a show that originated in The Netherlands.

Get into the swing

— Wynton Marsalis, Trumpeter, composer, bandleader on the leadership lessons of jazz

- ✓ Respect the abilities of others. Listen to each other. Trust. Make adjustments and improvise based on what others do.

- ✓ When people trust each other they work for the common good. They are in sync and prepared for anything.

- ✓ Drummer Elvin Jones articulated it well: "In order to play with somebody on a profound level, you have to be willing to die with them." That's jazz.

- ✓ Lack of integrity is the biggest threat to jazz – or business.

- ✓ Swing is a rhythm. When a company swings it is able to absorb mediocre and poor decisions.

"Swing is the feeling that our way is more important than my way."

✓ Swing is the objective. It makes us want to work together.

✓ A swing philosophy extends to audiences, consumers, staff or dysfunctional families. Proceed by feel like a church congregation reciting together and unrehearsed.

✓ Unleash creativity and spontaneity by being authentic. Inauthentic people are technical. They lack feeling. People are inauthentic when they haven't paid their dues.

"A business that swings will be successful."

✓ Don't act like what you are. Be what you are. Value your ideas, mine your dreams. Be creative inside or outside of tradition. Outside, create a new world. Inside, create a new way of doing old things better. Reinvigorate a tradition, or counter-state it.

✓ Embrace differences. Innovators see how things that appear to be opposites are in fact the same.

"Everybody knows church music and whorehouse songs. But we don't have the courage to put two opposites together."

- ✓ A business is like a group of jazz musicians organized under the extreme pressure of time. People won't get along, but they should always try.

- ✓ Leaders mature. Children are responsible for themselves. Adults are responsible to families, neighborhoods, communities, country and world. Ascension to maturity is tied to responsibility and the magnitude of what we choose to take on. This ladder leads from personal artistry to humanity itself.

- ✓ Jazz is the most flexible art form in the history of the planet because it believes in individuals. It believes in the human power to create wonderful things, and it embraces that instead of attempting to administrate it away with senseless titles and useless hierarchies.

Did you know?

- Marsalis got his first trumpet at age 8. By 14, he was invited to perform with the New Orleans Philharmonic.

- Entered The Juilliard School in New York in 1979 to study classical trumpet but left to pursue jazz. In 1997 became the first jazz artist to receive the Pulitzer Prize in music.

- Only artist to win Grammy Awards in both classical and jazz.

- Named one of America's Best Leaders by Harvard's Kennedy School of Government.

Wrangling for business

— **Mackey McDonald, VF CEO 1996-2006 on branding and marketing**

✓ Consumers are both emotional and rational. The statement made by a man who wears Wrangler jeans is that he is practical, down-to-earth and value-driven. Some buy for comfort, some for value, some are looking to appeal to the opposite sex.

✓ Build lines into different activities. Jeans are worn while camping, skateboarding and going to church. North Face is for mountain climbers and those in Central Park who wish they were mountain climbing.

✓ Subscribe to services that provide information on fads and trends. Talk to people to get inside their heads. Why do people skateboard? What needs aren't being met? Marketing is science.

"Lifestyles drive trends, not movie stars."

✓ To compete with Amazon, retailers will have a greater selection, but they won't have the inventory for people to walk out of the store with their purchases. Merchandise will be shipped to their home in hours or days. Buyers want to see what apparel feels like and how it looks.

✓ A J.C. Penney store near a college campus should have a much different mix of products than a store in the suburbs.

Did you know?

- McDonald was an observation pilot in Vietnam.

- Wore jeans to work, size 36/32. He put a sports coat on to dress up.

- Golf handicap: 15. Favorite course: Augusta.

- VF is a giant Fortune 500 apparel company that owns Wrangler, Lee, Rustlers, JanSport, Lucy, The North Face, Timberland and others.

Pointers from across the pond

— Nancy McKinstry, Wolters Kluwer CEO 2003-present on business in Europe

- ✓ The U.S. system works in America, and the Dutch system works in the Netherlands. Global organizations create hybrid systems that blend across borders.

- ✓ English, already the language of business, has been made more so by the Internet.

- ✓ European executives like to talk politics, economics and culture. Discuss only business at lunch and you won't be invited back.

- ✓ America has more female executives than Europe. Contrary to beliefs, it's easier in the U.S. for women to combine a career and family.

"Schools don't provide lunches. Parents, usually mothers, pick their children up an lunchtime. Stores close early and don't open on Sundays, which makes it difficult for working mothers."

✓ European companies are more formal. Executives aren't addressed by first names. The phrase, "our company is aggressive," has a negative connotation.

✓ Europe is not one market. Cultures vary from country to country. Use local management on the ground. A big challenge is finding managers with a local mindset and global expertise.

✓ There are more similarities between the U.S., Germany and Holland than there are between those countries and Southern Europe, where decision-making is more collaborative, and long-term business relationships are essential to success.

✓ Create enough flexibility in the labor force to manage the peaks and valleys in business. This is more difficult in Europe because of regulations regarding layoffs.

✓ Employees everywhere are generally committed to getting the job done, regardless of geography or culture.

✓ European and U.S. companies will focus more on China and Asia going forward.

Did you know?

- McKinstry runs, bikes and golfs.

- Born in Connecticut. Favorite vacation spots: Bailey Island, Maine and Paris.

- Her husband, an anesthesiologist, commutes to his job in New York.

Throwing a Hail Mary

— Joe Moglia, TD Ameritrade CEO 2001-08 on the leadership lessons of football

✓ Football teams have losing seasons from time to time. That's seldom an option in business.

✓ In football and business, a loss is more painful than a win is gratifying. A football game is more emotional, but a season is equivalent to a year of running a firm.

✓ Analyze the odds of success and what happens if the plan fails. Don't forget to assess the risk of being wrong.

✓ There's no risk in a Hail Mary pass. That's a last-ditch effort. Business risk is more like an all-out blitz. Prepare and analyze to know tendencies of yourself and the opponent.

✓ The book Perimeter Attack Offense describes how to attack the cornerback, safety and outside linebacker. Those players have dual run-pass responsibilities. The key is to make those players hesitate, even for a fraction of a second, to give a two- or three-inch advantage to the offense. Create similar advantages in business, such as technology, to give your team an edge.

✓ In football and business, when you come up against a team of equal or greater strength, you need a scheme to outplay them. If your scheme is better on paper but you can't execute, you'll lose.

✓ The most ingenious game plans fail if no one is blocking and tackling. When two teams execute, the team with a better game plan wins.

"To succeed, you need four qualities: spiritual soundness, dedication, courage and love."

✓ Love is the willingness to sacrifice for the betterment of others – the team, the organization. It's not the emotions you feel when you ask your wife to marry you.

✓ Spiritual soundness is the ability to have peace of mind, to be comfortable with who you are, understand your strengths and acknowledge your weaknesses. It's a comfort level with yourself.

✓ In football and business there are star performers. Convince the stars that the only way to succeed is to reach team goals.

"It's no good to lead the team in scoring if the team doesn't make the playoffs."

✓ The star quarterback won't be effective if he's on the ground due to lousy protection. In business, if your star running back doesn't recognize the importance of his blockers, you need another back.

✓ You can have good athletes playing the wrong position. Move underperforming employees to where they can be successful.

Did you know?

- Moglia quit as TD Ameritrade CEO to become head coach at Coastal Carolina. Collegiate record: 51-15.

- High school and college football coach for 16 years before joining Merrill Lynch in 1984. Top broker by 1988.

- First stock: Chrysler, bought at age 19. Lost money.

Leadership lessons of the nuns

— Thomas Monaghan, Domino's Pizza founder on how to juggle faith, wealth and politics

- ✓ If you want to be successful over a long period, have an idea why you were born and what life is about. Nobody can function without thinking that through.

- ✓ Live by Christ's teachings. Be a straight arrow.

- ✓ Nuns teach that honesty is the best policy. Treat suppliers fairly, teach the golden rule to your people. The idea of cheating on your wife should be unthinkable.

"Surveys show that the most religious profession is the military. Businessmen are No. 2. The media are at the bottom."

- ✓ The word bankruptcy should not be in the vocabulary. If you're hopelessly insolvent, pay every dollar you owe.

- ✓ When people trust you, all you need is a handshake.

✓ Strong families provide a foundation from which to operate a business. Some ignore their families, are workaholics and never home. They have no purpose in life, which will eventually hurt the business.

✓ Money is neutral. It prints Bibles and pays for priests, hospitals, orphanages and soup kitchens.

"The nuns told us that money was the root of all evil. But it's the love of money that's the root of all evil."

✓ Don't live like a pauper, but don't engage in ostentatious things. Simplify life. No more airplanes, no more yachts. It's a big relief.

✓ Read *Mere Christianity* by C.S. Lewis.

✓ Wealthy or not, put God first. Pray to God to ask his will for you. Listen and follow.

"Dominos had franchisees near college campuses who thought they were injured by my pro-life position, but it helped business more than it hurt. For every customer lost, we gained many."

✓ Pride is the greatest of sins. You're a successful capitalist if you've served other people, you've served your employees, you've served your customers. Don't create an empire and an imperial life.

✓ Faith doesn't cause war. War is hunger for power. Extremists use religion to justify atrocities.

✓ Most customers don't care about controversy.

"I don't consider myself a liberal or a conservative. I'm for free enterprise, small government, less taxes. I'm a believer in the plight of minorities. The Earth was created for our use and not abuse."

✓ Become rich by seeing that rich is not important. If you were brought up poor and embarrassed by holes in your shoes, get that out of your system.

✓ Getting rich is enjoyable. Giving it away, fulfilling.

Did you know?

- Monaghan grew up in foster homes and a Catholic orphanage after his father died on Christmas Eve 1941. He was 4. His mother decided she could not take care of her two sons.

- Founded Domino's with brother James, who traded his share for a Volkswagen Beetle.

- Wanted to be a priest as far back as the second grade. Dismissed from the seminary for being too mischievous, but says the real reason was because he did not write home enough.

- Met his wife while delivering a pizza.

- Sold Domino's in 1998 for $1 billion. Bought antique cars, yachts and the Detroit Tigers baseball team. Says he is now invested "in helping people get to heaven," through the Ave Maria Foundation.

What comes down must go up

— James Morgan, Applied Materials CEO 1977-2003 on leading through economic slumps

- ✓ Downturns once trickled in gradually over a couple of quarters. Everybody has the same information now, and that leads to abrupt ups and downs. Don't be a deer in the headlights. Things unravel quickly. Develop the skill of anticipation.

"Problems show up like rocks in a bay when the tide is out."

- ✓ Develop a navigation plan. When the water is up, you don't know where the rocks are. Use downturns to improve.

- ✓ Recessions are different, but the response is similar. Shrink travel, inventories and population.

- ✓ Get bad news out of the way early: pay cuts, days off without pay. Layoffs are painful. Rip the Band-Aid and get everyone focused.

✓ Instruct managers to meet with employees worldwide. Give an explanation for what happened, why and what the near-term outlook is going to be.

✓ Communicate so that there will be no surprises if business doesn't pick up. Give employees reason to trust information that comes from management. Spell out what it will take to get through the tough period.

✓ Prepare for the upswing during tough times. Focus on long-term strategy. Build a strong balance sheet that leads you to take risks. Employees and investors want to believe in a solid plan. Spend on research and development. Get new products out.

"Like in football, this is the time to establish good field position."

✓ Catch competitors off guard and get a big play.

✓ Good people are available in recessions. Look for strategic hires. Avoid laying off talented workers, and continue with a college graduate hiring program.

"Great companies are built in tough times."

✓ In good times, scramble to keep up with demand. In bad times, get close to your customers. Make sure you know what they want, what they need.

Did you know?

- Morgan's wife Becky Morgan was a California state senator for nine years.

- Has a pond with koi, ornamental Japanese fish. Avid skier.

Give choking companies the Heimlich maneuver

— Anne Mulcahy, Xerox CEO 2001-09 on leading through a disaster

✓ When a company's in trouble, customers and employees need to see quick action. Make commitments, execute, build credibility. Don't disappoint.

✓ Be decisive. Even with an incredible brand, people don't have unending patience.

✓ When there's no growth in the industry, focus on pirating business from competitors.

✓ Shareholders used to receive a separate message but communication has become aligned in a world of transparency. Employees stay with the company for the same reasons investors invest and customers choose to be patrons. Convince all stakeholders that you're competitive and best in class and a leader in the marketplace.

"We retained our research and development expenses of 5% to 6% of revenue. In the last six quarters we introduced 27 new products. We refreshed our whole portfolio"

✓ Research often brings ideas that aren't a good fit. License that technology.

✓ Customers want relevant products. They won't pay for anything they don't consider to be of value. Offer options without bells and whistles.

✓ Demonstrate that your products save time or money.

✓ Beware of emotional attachments. Xerox all but abandoned the copy business. Stay adaptive.

Did you know?

• Mulcahy took over at Xerox when the company was $17 billion in debt and in the middle of an accounting scandal.

• Grew up with four brothers and says she learned to embrace competition.

• In 2002, Xerox's 700 patents put it among the top 10.

When a new product gives customers a heart attack

— James Mullen, Biogen CEO 2000-10 on marching through disaster

✓ Nothing in business is more risky than drug development and it stays fraught through the life of the product. Even with FDA approval, drug companies have limited information on side effects down the road.

✓ If something might be unsafe, let the rope out gradually. It doesn't matter if you are a biotech company or Chipotle.

✓ To avoid a Vioxx-like disaster, stay ever-alert. Have safeguards in place for the integrity of the organization.

✓ Understand complexity. Knowledge accumulates at a dizzying pace. It will be a long time before that turns around.

"The human genome project has accelerated information 100-fold in 10 years."

✓ It's called research and development because the answer is unknown at the start. A negative result is valuable if it tells you what path not to follow.

✓ If innovation requires failure, don't blame innovators who fail. Avoid self-inflicted failure.

✓ Learn from mistakes and broadcast them throughout the organization so they aren't repeated.

✓ Cost, quality and speed are at odds with each other. Start with quality, then achieve a quick timeline and trim costs.

✓ Think things through, measure what you do, find root causes of problems, correct them, and don't do it again.

✓ Keep a balance between having defined ground rules and a culture where researchers can poke around. That's how great discoveries are made. But they can't be turned loose to bark up any tree.

✓ Recruit researchers with a curiosity to learn what's going on in other disciplines such as patent law or the manufacturing process.

✓ All employees want to know what they're supposed to be doing, how their work is measured. That's more important to knowledge workers.

✓ It's easy to tell if applicants have the technical skill and experience to perform a job. It's tougher to determine if they are going to be a great contributor and collaborator and function on a team. Spend time interviewing for those aspects.

"I hired a German sales force without understanding five words of German. I picked out the best reps by watching how they interacted with their peers, the body language and the rest."

✓ Guard against the "not invented here" syndrome. It's critical to look outward for ideas.

✓ CEOs don't have to be innovative. They have to be good at spotting ideas and creating the environment for those ideas to be tested.

✓ Innovation requires incentives. If a drug company is expected to give away a cure for AIDS, then a cure for baldness will more likely be invented.

Did you know?

- Mullen planned on becoming a medical doctor when he got to college, but wanted to use science to solve problems.

- It takes $1 billion and 15 years to develop the average new drug. One in 1,000 compounds tested makes it to human trials, and one in five of those emerges as a drug.

- Greatest breakthrough in medical history: "It's still penicillin."

Overcoming resistance to change

— Bob Nardelli, Home Depot CEO 2000-07 on taking over a successful company

✓ Resist the urge to stay in the past. General Electric was once on a pedestal like Google, Apple and Amazon today. Change is the only constant.

✓ Like a football team after a Sunday game, study film. Find deficiencies and figure out how to fix them.

"If you can fix it with an existing player, then do. Otherwise, get a new quarterback, right?"

✓ Combat the resistance with compassion. Companies have a proud past and employees don't want people coming in to "fix what's broken." From their point of view, nothing is broken.

"The culture at Home Depot was embracing. They knew each other, they grew up together, they toiled together, they won together. I was an unknown, an aberration."

- ✓ Be human, visible, approachable. Meet everyone. Practice deep immersion. Try to gain confidence early on.

- ✓ Expect a landscape strewn with people who are arrogantly or belligerently dug in and unwilling to listen. Expect resistance and upheaval in certain areas.

- ✓ Expect some to say, "No way, I'm going to leave." Expect others to say, "I agree that we need a strategic change, but I don't want to go through it and I'm going to leave." Some will say, "I'm with you. I want to help." Lastly, some will say, "I'm going to stick around because you, too, will pass."

"The more you talk about the strategy, the better. Of course, success helps."

- ✓ The biggest mistake is doing nothing.

- ✓ Enhance the core, extend the business and expand the market. These three E's provide consistency and a calming effect.

✓ Some see such strategies as the flavor of the month. They put it under the category of banners and bull. Rightfully so. Change comes through consistency and resolve and the unwavering articulation of a strategy.

Did you know?

- Nardelli was an average student, a star athlete, an altar boy, a Boy Scout, class officer, yearbook editor and ROTC cadet. Dreamed of playing in the NFL.

- Transformed GE Power Systems into a $20-billion-a-year unit. In 2000, lost a three-way race to replace retiring Jack Welch as GE CEO.

When the inmates run the asylum

— Vineet Nayar, HCL Technologies CEO 2007-13 on worker democracy

- ✓ Command-and-control is the easiest management style. It's not the most productive. The democratic, accountability model is difficult, it weighs heavy on management, but it's productive.

- ✓ India is the world's largest democracy, but it's easier to introduce workplace democracy in Europe and the USA.

"In India we control our kids until age 27. We run their lives until they get married. As a society, the U.S. is more open to workplace democracy."

- ✓ When management became more accountable to shareholders, companies became better. It didn't create chaos, it created value. Shareholders don't tell businesses what to do, but there's more accountability.

- ✓ The same principle applies to workplace democracy, especially in knowledge businesses.

- ✓ Bosses can't be voted out by the rank and file. However, management's duty is to serve the workers just as elected officials are there to serve the public.

"Nelson Mandela and other great political leaders understood that their job was to enable people to find their own destiny."

- ✓ Corporate democracy isn't a recipe for anarchy and chaos. Don't destroy the hierarchy. Increase the accountability of leadership to employees.

- ✓ Employees can open a trouble ticket on anyone in the company, on a manager, on anyone. A response is required.

- ✓ Don't permit certain departments to become gods in an organization, don't permit fiefdoms.

- ✓ As CEO, own up to personal weaknesses. Make your 360-degree feedback public to all employees. Encourage senior managers to do the same. Leaders must overcome the fear of having their flaws exposed.

- ✓ The mantra is no longer "the customer is always right." Employees create value for the customer.

Customers patronize companies where employees are most important.

"When I travel on an airline, it's not the CEO who makes a difference."

✓ Democratic companies fire under-performers. People are given more opportunities to succeed, but the outcome for slackers is the same.

✓ Managers who get negative feedback gravitate to other jobs. Inside the system of democracy, they come to know they are bad managers.

✓ Good managers will remain to nurture employees and allow them to create more value.

Did you know?

• Nayar joined HCL as a management trainee in 1985. Holds bachelor's degree in technology from G.B. Pant University ('83), and an MBA from XLRI-Jamshedpur ('85). Both schools are in India.

• Likes adventure sports. Has done glacier trekking in Europe and New Zealand. Favorite scuba destination: Hawaii.

When a food fight is in order

— Clarence Otis, Darden Restaurants CEO 2004-13 on gaining market share when the pie shrinks

✓ Resist reducing the staff if it erodes the customer experience. In a recession, people dine out less. An anniversary or birthday is more dear. Don't leave a bad taste in mouths.

✓ Consumers return when the economy improves, but they'll long remember a bad experience.

✓ Pay attention to companies outside your industry. Walmart has the supply chain. Marriott has brands that are positioned differently. The auto companies have a range of models from entry level to mid-tier to luxury. Do the same. Emphasize value in a recession.

"Companies that win position themselves to serve customers and strengthen their offer."

✓ There's risk in putting products on sale. It becomes the price customers expect to pay. Pump out coupons and lose the ability to command a regular price.

✓ Good employees stay longer during recessions. Take advantage of that. Deemphasize new employee training and layer on advanced training and development.

✓ It's a good time to replace under-performing workers.

Did you know?

- Otis is the son of a janitor, and homemaker. Read almost every novel and biography at the public library in Watts by the ninth grade.

- Received the Horatio Alger Award, which recognizes individuals who overcome adversity to achieve.

- When he became CEO of Darden Restaurants in 2004, he was one of eight African Americans ever to be chairman and/or CEO of a Fortune 500 company.

- Owns one of the USA's leading private collections of African-American art.

- Darden Restaurants has more than 1,500 restaurant locations and more than 150,000 employees, making it the world's largest full-service restaurant company with brands like Olive Garden and LongHorn Steakhouse.

Reject 99 out of 100 opportunities

Jeff Rich, Affiliated Computer Services CEO 1989-2005 on the discipline of M&A

- ✓ There are a zillion reasons to reject a deal. An overpriced company, unhappy employees, an unmotivated workforce, deteriorating financial conditions, a management team that wants to cash out.

"Walk away if anything makes you feel uncomfortable in your tummy."

- ✓ Guard your ego. Those who have to prevail overpay. Those who want only to run a bigger company – not a more profitable one – fail.

- ✓ The best time to buy anything, including companies, is when no one else is. There aren't a lot of sellers at depressed prices, but be patient. If prices stay down, financial pressure to sell builds.

- ✓ Have your people stake out acquisition candidates. Watch the lobby from the parking lot before and after closing. Do people get to work early and leave late? Are they stampeding out the door at 4:30, or is there a steady stream that starts at 5 and ends at 7 or 8 or 9?

"Is there a work ethic, or does it run like a bureaucracy?"

- ✓ Synergy is over-rated. It's OK to identify cost savings and revenue opportunities, but synergy is often pure dumb luck.

- ✓ Beware when the management team wants millions to put in the bank. It's OK to give them a little money to tuck away, but make sure they're motivated to stay and do good things.

- ✓ Everyone should be smiling when closing the deal. Beware if someone is unhappy.

- ✓ Acquisitions lead to job cuts. Be straightforward about that. Mergers are healthy for the economy and lower the cost of delivering a product. People accept the truth, but they won't accept uncertainty, or evasiveness.

"The stupidest thing a CEO can do when there's a merger is stand up and say 'nothing is changing.'"

✓ A lot of acquisitions fail for two reasons: Buyers overpay, or there is a poor cultural fit. Anyone can buy. The hard part is integration.

✓ Cultural fit means the two organizations must share the same purpose, the same operating philosophy.

✓ Sometimes they just don't like each other. The AOL-Time Warner merger went bad due to a clash. Beware of East meets West, dot-com millionaire meets corporate lifers.

✓ The two merged companies can't have different pay scales.

✓ Have senior people at the new company rank all other senior executives. Are they A, B or C players? Identify the clear winners and losers.

✓ Watch retention. If good people start to leave, expect problems in sales, client satisfaction and, ultimately, financial performance.

✓   Advice to employees: Expect job cuts, a lot of cuts if the merger is with a direct competitor.

✓   Each employee must find out what's happening to the company, their division and themselves personally. This is a free market for labor, and those who don't feel secure, should take action and find another job.

Did you know?

- Rich had completed 66 transactions by 2003. Affiliated Computer Services was itself acquired by Xerox in 2010.

- A high school hockey star, quarterback for the Goodrich High School Martians football team.

- Raced in the "Hotter Than Hell 100" bike race in Texas, has ridden cross-country on a Harley, rafted on Costa Rican rivers, climbed 14,265-foot Castle Peak in Colorado.

Don't let our daughters dumb down

Sally Ride, first American woman in space 1983 on keeping girls interested in math and science

✓ Don't succumb to stereotypes. Take encouragement from parents, teachers, counselors, anyone who says "science is for girls."

✓ It starts in sixth, seventh and eighth grade. If a girl dumbs down, it will probably be in middle school.

✓ Consider attending an all-girl high school. It can build confidence.

✓ Introduce a girl to the coolest female engineer at your company. Let them know that not every scientist is a 65-year-old guy with a lab coat and pocket protector and looks like Einstein.

✓ Show them the cool things that they can do in engineering.

✓ There are obvious differences between men and women. But in 1970, law school was 5% female, med school was 8% and business school was 4%. You could have concluded that women don't make good lawyers or doctors.

"Years ago, women were rare in national orchestras. One explanation was that they had less wind power. They did blind auditions and the number of women increased."

✓ It's hard to do gender-blind hiring. Do gender-blind initial screening. Managers can be made aware that they have preconceptions.

✓ Businesses that want good female employees should be involved in education even if educators object. Competition is good, vouchers should be considered, as should anything that holds the schools' feet to the fire.

✓ On the job, there can be very serious forms of discrimination for which there is legal redress. There are more subtle forms that women might not notice or think about until they accumulate over time. Use judgment. Sometimes it's best to take the high road, have a little sense of humor and let things roll off your back.

✓ We have a problem with boys, too. Seventy percent of the D's and F's are given to boys, and they account for 80 percent of dropouts. Women now earn more graduate degrees.

"You can work on two problems at once. You don't stop research on breast cancer because heart disease is so deadly."

Did you know?

- Ride's worst school subject was seventh-grade home economics, when it was required of girls.

"Can you imagine having to cook and eat tuna casserole at 8 a.m.?"

- Still the youngest American (32) in space.

- Attended Westlake School for Girls on a tennis scholarship. Achieved national ranking. Considered professional tennis.

- Died of pancreatic cancer in 2012.

Still more to do

Rachel Robinson, widow of Jackie Robinson on the state of corporate diversity

- ✓ There have been African-American CEOs such as Richard Parsons, Clarence Otis, Kenneth Chennault, Rodney O'Neal, Ursula Burns – Barack Obama – but opportunity in the ranks remains unequal.

- ✓ Young African-Americans know who runs companies, how often people get promoted, if there are salary gaps. Some take on a challenge, but most avoid hostile environments. The interaction between people at a workplace has an impact on productivity. Those who feel a part of the operation and are respected by colleagues do better.

- ✓ Advice to new hires: Develop a strong presence to succeed, yet don't be arrogant. Jackie Robinson was fundamentally a humble person, he had a deep spiritual depth and a belief in God. He was aggressive on the field. Off the field, he was a different person.

✓ Use various characteristics in different situations.

✓ Some companies and people give diversity lip service. Others are sincere, just as there were those who attacked Jackie Robinson, and others who rooted for him in a big way.

"Jackie excelled to show them that they were wrong. He knew he had to meet the challenge for our race."

✓ African-Americans should not get special favor once they're on the job. Then, it's up to them to produce. Neither should they be dismissed or treated poorly.

✓ Some fast-food restaurants have an all African-American staff at one location and all-Hispanic at another. Airlines staff planes with flight attendants who are all young, or all middle-aged. That can reduce problems in communication. It's positive unless it's used to shut others out or close opportunities. It's a good tactic if used to keep things harmonious.

Did you know?

- Rachel Annetta Isum met Jackie Robinson in 1941 at UCLA. They have fifteen grandchildren.

- Career nurse, primarily for the mentally ill. Named assistant professor of nursing at Yale, 1965.

- Jackie played for Brooklyn Dodgers 1947-56. Inducted into Hall of Fame, 1962. Died in 1972 at 53.

Never, never, never settle

T.J. Rodgers, Cypress Semiconductor founder on fighting lawsuits

✓ Class-action lawyers get up in the morning and look for stocks that have gone down. They sue. They will go away for $8 million, or cost you $1 million in legal fees looking for a smoking-gun memo.

✓ 90% of companies settle to get it behind them, which has created a thriving corporate litigation industry. Don't give away money if you're innocent.

✓ Don't capitulate to profiteers. Don't be an easy target.

"Porcupine is a bad lunch."

✓ Pay up if the suit has merit. Otherwise, settling is the same as paying ransom to kidnappers except that fighting lawsuits is easier because nobody's life is at stake – only money.

✓ Lawyers advise burning documentation and deleting email. That's wrong advice. Keep it all and let opposing lawyers go fishing. They can talk in court about the inch of bad stuff, but you can take a week talking about the good.

✓ CEOs should get deeply involved in trials. The minute a CEO lets lawyers make the decisions, the company is being run by a rookie, surrogate CEO. A lawsuit is a corporate action and unless you bring all disciplines and intelligence of the company, you're probably going to lose.

✓ Trust juries but be prepared to educate them. There can be bad verdicts, but it's worth the risk.

"Trials can create damaging publicity, but the minute we abandon fact and law, we're cavemen.

✓ Have a "mom" policy, which means explain the company to juries and potential shareholders as if they were your mothers. If mom wanted to invest, we wouldn't just give her the minimum information required by the Securities and Exchange Commission. We'd tell her again and again until she understood.

✓ Lobby for the British system, where the loser pays legal expenses.

Did you know that Rodgers likes to opine. A sample:

- Taxing the one percent moves money and investment decisions away from proven job producers to Washington amateurs.

- Corporate welfare should end.

- Washington is the enemy of Silicon Valley.

- Immigration is not a zero-sum game. Skilled immigrants don't take jobs from U.S. natives, they create them.

- Diversity should be achieved through the pursuit of talent no matter what package it comes in.

- Interest rates should be decided by computer, not by the humans of the Federal Reserve.

Be Krafty

Irene Rosenfeld, Kraft Foods CEO 2006-11 on taking charge in a transition

- ✓ Lead from the head and the heart.

- ✓ Come up with a mission statement like "Making today delicious." The statement is a powerful rallying cry.

- ✓ Encourage employees to act like owners. Have them spend money like it's their own. Cost cutting should be a means to an end – and that end is growth.

- ✓ An owner doesn't have the time to sit in a meeting going through 100 pages of documents, so neither should workers. Keep it simple. Be nimble.

"It's hard to get up every morning and say "Cut this cost." You need to feel like your work has a higher purpose."

- ✓ Some employees will like the company's new direction and will be prepared to follow. Promote them. Replace the others with outsiders.

"Make changes with new blood."

✓ Have a passion to win and a sense of urgency about getting it done.

✓ At the end of the day, it's about balance. Extremes are rarely the right answer.

Did you know?

- Rosenfeld was once No. 6 on the *Forbes* list of the 100 most powerful women among business executives.

- Became CEO of Kraft in 2006, which became a Fortune 100 company in 2008 when it was spun off by Altria Group.

- Rollerblades.

- Straightens the cookie shelves when grocery shopping.

Skin in the game

Ron Sargent, Staples CEO 2002-16 on beefing up the board

- ✓ Great companies require good governance. Directors need a nuts-and-bolts understanding of the business. They need to challenge management. They need a healthy balance between loyalty and independence.

- ✓ Elect directors with good values, broad-based experience with different backgrounds and perspectives.

"You can't legislate morality. Money does not trump integrity."

- ✓ Boards have an obligation to claw back incentive pay if the company's results were overstated.

- ✓ Require directors to own a $200,000 stake in company stock to align their interests with shareholders.

✓ Director pay should be competitive. Companies that pay on the far end of the bell curve should be scrutinized.

✓ Pay more to committee chairmen and to those who attend more meetings. Unfair treatment impedes board dynamics.

✓ Directors have additional responsibilities relating to Sarbanes-Oxley.

✓ Transparency is valuable, but Sarbanes-Oxley was an overreaction to bad actors in a few companies. The expense is too much of a burden on small and medium companies. They may be better off being private.

"Sarbanes-Oxley cost Staples $1 million to comply."

✓ Sarbanes-Oxley makes honest companies jump through more regulatory hoops, yet does not stop executives who are intent on being corrupt. If someone is determined to commit fraud, it can be done with or without the legislation.

✓ Advice to investors: Don't focus on company governance. Look at the industry and track record of current management more than at the board. The management team is living with the company 60 hours a week.

Did you know?

- Sargent was born in Fort Thomas, Kentucky. MBA at age 23 from Harvard Business School.

- Started out at 16 stocking shelves for grocery store chain Kroger. Worked 10 years for Kroger before joining Staples in 1989.

Are your employees well-trained seals?

Julie Scardina, SeaWorld animal ambassador on the secrets of positive feedback

✓ Don't take your whale's compliance, motivation or energy for granted. Use effective communication, encouragement, rewards, creativity, effort and variety. Pay attention to good behavior. Don't make a big issue of their mistakes.

✓ Set your dolphins up to succeed. Reward them sometimes for nothing more than a great attitude.

"Work hard to create an environment that is interesting, fun, stimulating. Draw attention to behavior you want repeated."

✓ Don't punish. Go neutral. Inattention is effective discipline. Punishment has a dampening effect, which can lead to defensiveness and aggression. Give misbehaving dolphins a couple of hours to hang out by themselves.

✓ Say, there are four animals in your pool. You send them all out on a job and one of them says: "Ehhh, I'm going over to talk to the whale at the coffee pot." The last thing you want to do is leave the three whales that do the right thing and give attention to the time waster.

✓ Where do you devote time and effort? Devote it to the mammals doing the right thing.

✓ If the whales aren't getting it, trainers haven't been positive enough, or the whales haven't developed enough.

✓ Trainers never view themselves as a boss, especially when dealing with whales.

'I'm 110 pounds and get into the water with 10,000-pound killer whales. The last thing I want is a whale to be thinking: "You know, yesterday, she told me that I wasn't doing a very good job."

✓ Avoid feedback that is intermittent or vague. You want your whale to be thinking: "We had fun yesterday, even though I wasn't quite understanding what you wanted. I'm ready to try again."

✓ Don't give fake praise. What you reinforce is what you get.

✓ Fish is not the reward of choice for whales and dolphins. Each animal has its own favorites. Be creative. It can be toys of different sizes, different colors of ice cubes that melt in different ways that they chew, swallow or push around and watch melt. They like being touched, scratched or rubbed. Variety is important.

✓ Mammals become satiated with rewards that they get over and over. We all like to get back rubs. But if somebody gave us ten back rubs a day, we'd want something else. Keep it fresh.

✓ An overused reward for humans is money.

✓ When you ask a whale to breach and splash the audience, the best time to reward him is at the apex of his behavior. But it's impossible to reward him when he's up in the air. Use a communication "bridge." Blow a whistle to tell him he is going to get the reward.

✓ A "bridge" for human mammals is praise.

✓ Submissive whales go, "Uh-oh, the dominant whale's looking at me funny. I'm dropping my fish, or I'm not going to play with that toy." Teach the dominant animals that they need to be kind to less aggressive animals if they want to get reinforced.

✓ Treat all animals with respect. No one incident of bad behavior is worth losing a close relationship over.

✓ Competency comes from the right mix of success and challenges, failure and encouragement. Notice good behavior, ignore the bad. If you are dishing out discipline or punishment, you're wrong.

Did you know?

- Scardina was the most frequent guest on *The Tonight Show* with Jay Leno.

- Allergic to fish. "I can handle it and feed it to the whales, but I can't eat it."

- Her pets included a blind rescue parrot from the Amazon.

The big gorillas in the room

Henry Silverman, Cendant CEO 1991-2006 on debt and taxes

✓ Deficits are OK if they are around 2% of GDP.

✓ Pork, government waste and corporate welfare are small potatoes compared with Social Security, Medicare and Medicaid.

✓ Those who try to fix entitlements are like the first person trying to twist the cap off a ketchup bottle. The air seal is tough, and you get red in the face. Eventually, someone will take the cap off, and we'll say, "Gosh, you must be lifting weights." But it will be because others have incrementally loosened the cap.

"Someone must start twisting the cap."

✓ Entitlement reform requires difficult decisions. If you have a stroke in the U.K. they send you home.

✓ Every idea faces opposition. Like ending the home mortgage deduction. Only 24% claim it, but it might hurt all home owners by depressing real estate values.

✓ Technology can save $140 billion in health care.

✓ We need to reform our medical liability system. Americans need to become smarter consumers by understanding the cost and quality of care.

"The advice I give the President is, you have to start somewhere. He may not succeed, but he can get it started for the next guy, or the next guy after that."

✓ Debt undermines our global competitiveness.

✓ Taxes are a necessary evil, but if entitlements aren't reduced, taxes will rise drastically. That will devastate economic growth. It's a death spiral.

✓ Taking away a tax deduction is a tax increase.

✓ The source of economic growth is the private sector. Growth creates jobs. Companies pay taxes, and their employees pay taxes.

✓ Therefore, let a consensus form in the business community over proposals that strengthen the economy.

"Solve the deficit by growing out of it."

- Companies are at odds over solutions. Cendant is in the rental car business and has a different perspective about insurance matters than Allstate.

Did you know?

- Silverman's childhood dream was to play center field for the Yankees, but he couldn't hit a curve.

Don't shame companies for making money

Bruce Smith, Tesoro CEO 1996-2010 on being the corporate villain

- ✓ Most people frown when gasoline prices go up, but a lot of jobs are created by the industry.

- ✓ The free market is efficient. Price-gouging is a common criticism, but very rare in practice.

"The Bill of Rights does not say 'life, liberty, the pursuit of happiness AND cheap gasoline."

- ✓ Companies ranging from Tesoro, Walmart and Google come under fire for being successful. Controversy can't be avoided. Be proactive. Practice honesty. Communicate, communicate, communicate.

- ✓ Educate employees so that they can defend where they work at social gatherings. They didn't cause hurricanes that shut down refineries in the Gulf.

✓ When oil prices rise, more oil will be found. That moderates the price.

✓ Every company wants to be seen as green, not brown. Make a sincere effort to demonstrate that when given the chance.

✓ Government regulation and interference has a poor track record. We keep imported ethanol out of the U.S. with a 54-cent tariff. Most people won't spend an extra $500 a year in hybrid car payments to save $200 on gas.

✓ The infrastructure is not set up for alternative fuel.

Did you know?

• Smith grew up in Coffeyville, Kan., population 16,000.

• Served in U.S. Army during the Vietnam War years, but never went to Vietnam.

• Hobbies include golf, skiing, tennis, reading and traveling with his wife and family. Golf handicap: 20. Favorite family vacation: skiing in Aspen, Colo.

The past points to the future

Fred Smith, FedEx founder on the leadership lessons of historical figures

✓ There aren't many new things under the sun. History lessons are clear and proven.

"Somebody once asked Chinese leader Zhou Enlai what he thought of the French Revolution. He said: 'It's too early to tell.'"

✓ Business successes are but blips in history. Tom Watson and his son were fantastic managers, but IBM's success waned. Now, it's General Electric's turn. Listen to history, not business gurus.

✓ Alexander the Great was better at winning the peace than at winning wars. He reached out after a military victory. Losers had always been put in shackles, or had their heads cut off. Alexander gave defeated chieftains authority.

✓ Likewise, most acquisitions result in wholesale turnover. Alexander's far-seeing management style enabled him to build the biggest empire ever, matched only by the Romans years later. His lesson: Make an acquired company a part of the team – make two plus two equal five.

✓ George Marshall was the architect of the reconstruction of Europe – the Marshall plan and the United Nations. He was self-effacing. He refused to write his memoirs because he said his memories had been paid for by taxpayers, and because the truth about some people would be unpleasant for their families. Learn humility from Marshall.

✓ Historic figures who would have made great CEOs: Marshall, Theodore Roosevelt, Peter Drucker and Cordell Hull. Hull was a congressman, senator and secretary of State under Franklin Roosevelt. He won the Nobel Peace Prize. He was the father of the modern trading system. After World War II, the Depression and the Smoot Hawley tariff increases, Hull became an advocate of open trade. Open markets track back to Hull just as all management theory comes from Drucker.

"Hull said, 'When goods cannot cross borders, armies will.'"

✓ Union Civil War Gen. George McClellan was fired, but too late. He was too cautious. He never had enough resources, always waited for the optimal moment. He was indecisive.

✓ Too many leaders think inaction is the least risky path when action can be the most conservative and safest. Before Pearl Harbor, they put all the airplanes in the middle of the airfield to protect them from saboteurs. We were undone by cautiousness, not bravado.

✓ Every decision is made with imperfect information. Washington was pretty sure when he crossed the Delaware that he was going to be annihilated. Eisenhower had rudimentary meteorological information when he made the D-Day decision on the 6th of June. He wrote out on a slip of paper that the fault of the invasion failing "is mine alone." History is the study of people going out on a limb.

✓ Great leaders take responsibility. When they have a chance to rectify a mistake, they react urgently and strongly, and oftentimes do things they don't want to do.

✓ Julius Caesar had a proconsul in Palestine, one in Gaul and one in Britain. Each reported to a cavalry commander, each had infantrymen, an archer, etc. FedEx has leaders in Hong Kong, Brussels, etc. Each has an IT person, each has a business unit head, each has a personnel person.

"Julius Caesar would recognize FedEx's organizational structure."

✓ Speed has been important throughout history. The Pony Express was the FedEx of its time. It was put out of business by the telegraph. FedEx sails the clipper ships of the computer age. We carry pharmaceuticals, fashion goods, surgical kits, airplane parts, semiconductors. High-value goods are more expensive to move slowly. Container ships move 98% of the tonnage. Air is less than 2%, but almost 45% of the value. Take out petroleum and agriculture and the majority of international trade doesn't go by sea.

- ✓ Business is fueled by the Internet. Order an auto part from the Sahara desert and in 24 to 48 hours it's there.

- ✓ Read history, not management books. A half dozen management books provide 95% of what you need to know about leadership. Know Edward Deming and J.M. Juran if you have an interest in providing a quality product. Drucker is profound in terms of the theory of business.

- ✓ The right war movies are valuable. *Twelve O'Clock High* with Gregory Peck is the story of a feeling man who has command of a unit, and he can't get the job done. The more he doesn't hold people accountable, the worse it becomes. He tries to be too good, and it works against his purpose. Peck comes in with a cold dose of discipline. The lesson is if you don't hold people to a high standard, organizations gravitate to the lowest common denominator.

- ✓ Leaders are made. Some people are incapable, but you can identify them on the front end. The rest can be taught to be effective. Some fail because leadership requires them to subordinate self-interests for the organization.

170

✓ A Mount Rushmore of CEOs would include Alfred Sloan of General Motors. Henry Ford owned the auto industry, but Sloan recognized that the country was becoming more affluent and marketing was more important. Tom Watson Jr. at IBM made the courageous decision down the path into computing and modern mainframe computers. William Allen of Boeing bet on the swept-wing jet that led his company's aerospace dominance. How could you not put Walmart's Sam Walton there? He allowed people of modest incomes to have a standard of living they never dreamed.

Did you know?

- Smith served in the U.S. Marine Corps 1966-70. Remains CEO of FedEx, which he founded in 1971.

- If he could travel back in time he would want to see the Napoleonic armies laid out at Waterloo; the Constitutional Convention in Philadelphia; ancient Rome.

Who would Smith rather have lunch with?

✓ Ulysses S. Grant or Robert E. Lee? "Lee. I suspect Grant was not a good conversationalist."

✓ Thomas Jefferson or Alexander Hamilton? "Probably Hamilton."

✓ Washington or Lincoln? "Wow. I guess Lincoln because of the scope of what he was managing. What Washington did was every bit as profound, but in scale a fraction of what Lincoln dealt with."

✓ Mahatma Gandhi or Martin Luther King Jr.? "I admire both, but I'd choose King. In many ways he sort of saved America."

- ✓ Lewis and Clark or Magellan? "Lewis and Clark. Magellan did a lot, but it must have been pretty damn boring out on that ship. He probably had only one or two good stories."

- ✓ Hitler or Stalin? "Neither. The depravity of the Stalin regime was every bit as bad as the Nazis; it just didn't get the exposure. I would pass."

(*Editor's note:* Fred Smith is a fan of the first draft of history. He reads five newspapers each day and calls them "the world's best bargain." I've published the historical novel *The Cremation of Sam McGee* set in the 1898 heyday of yellow journalism. It's the most interesting period of newspaper history, before radio, when it was common to read five newspapers a day. The novel's unreliable narrator is a New York reporter who fabricates front-page stories to start the Spanish-American War and boost circulation in a newspaper war between moguls Joseph Pulitzer and William Randolph Hearst. Request the first chapter at

https://caseystrikesout.wixsite.com/website).

When you're taking on water

Gary Smith, Ciena CEO 2001-present on leading through a catastrophe that sinks the ship

- ✓ Be paranoid. This is what can happen: In the late 1990s, Ciena was the hottest company around. It developed a way to boost the capacity of fiber-optic cables 40-fold. Orders poured in too fast to be filled, but it sold $1.5 billion of its core product in 2000. The next year, that plunged to $18 million. It lost a huge order from AT&T just as Ciena was to be acquired by Tellabs. The deal collapsed, and Ciena was wounded and alone.

- ✓ You wonder if you could have seen it coming. Dust yourself off and get galvanized around a plan. Notice little wins like getting a new customer or getting a new product to the same customers. Enjoy the baby steps as best you can.

"What doesn't kill you makes you stronger?"

✓   Paranoia provides energy and drive. Let it define the culture. Be paranoid even when times are great.

✓   When the company goes into shock, expect part of the leadership team to flee. Build trust with the rest. Look around the table and ask who wants to move forward.

✓   Be a victim or be proactive. Transformation is the no-option option.

✓   Remember, you're the micro in the macro. Don't bank on the tide going up. Be successful taking market share when the industry's stagnant.

✓   It's not just about market share, as high tech believes. Profits are important.

✓   You can't save your way to profitability. It takes three to five years to develop a new technology. If you're three-quarters of the way to a new product, do you waste all that investment, or do you continue until it's finished? I say continue. Outsource as much as you can. Time will tell.

✓ It's tough letting people go when it's no fault of their own. Be candid with the rank and file. You'd like to be able to say to people that this is the last layoff. But you can't.

✓ Pull it off and you'll look back on this and say it was a great achievement. Take personal satisfaction from the biggest challenge you've had.

Did you know?

- Smith was raised in the back country of England in a steel and mining area that he calls the Pittsburgh of the UK. His parents were factory workers.

- Met wife on a blind date in San Francisco and proposed to her at a castle in Wales.

- Completed a rugby game with a broken foot.

- Favorite flick: *Monty Python and the Holy Grail.*

The need for speed

Bobby Unser, Indy race car driver on running full throttle

✓ Go fast to win. Going fast means trying hard all the time in business, family life, sports.

✓ Running hard is a gamble. You won't finish as many races. But if you go fast, you'll be noticed.

"Lead the races. Winning will happen."

✓ Balance is important, but speed is a must. Go fast in practice, go fast in qualifications, don't be conservative. Go down in style and people will remember you. Mario and Michael Andretti have only one Indianapolis win between them, but they're as famous as any drivers on Earth. That's because they went fast and led.

✓ Don't put something off for a month. Get your facts lined up in a day or two and think something out in an hour.

✓ Keep yourself in shape, keep your mind clear. Be at a high state of alert.

✓ Learn from a wrong decision. If you lose, go home and think about why.

"You can tell a lot about someone by the effort they make when they fall down. Some people mope. Winners figure out what they did wrong and don't do it again."

✓ Don't go to work blank and fill in the day as it goes on. Plan your day, then be prepared for changes.

✓ Visualize your race. Visualize your competition, the racetrack, the weather. Somebody's going to win, somebody's going to lose. Visualize it all: the tires, the air pressure, the chassis. Don't be the guy who sits there and says, "I don't know how it's going to be," and then reacts.

✓ Go to sleep thinking about something you want to accomplish. The subconscious mind will work all night long for free.

"When I was 10, I went to bed dreaming of winning Pikes Peak. I'd go to sleep thinking about the road, turns to the left, turns to the right. By the time I was old enough to race, my subconscious mind had worked on it for years. I set all the records."

✓ The best drivers don't relax before a race. They don't go out to dinner the night before. They use the time to think.

✓ Some racers are born with tremendous talent, but no desire. If you have desire, manufacture what you need. Be better than the guy born with natural abilities. In business or motor sports, the guy who really wants to be a champion wins.

"I was on the high school wrestling team. Our biggest competitor was the blind school. Those guys couldn't see, but they could win. That's where I learned about desire."

✓ Wants are different than desires. You can sit on the couch sipping a beer and want something. If you desire to be the head of General Motors, you go to work in the automotive industry, not over in Africa searching for diamonds.

✓ There are different ways to win. Race differently if you have the fastest car. If your car is slower, push the envelope to find its limits.

✓ When the race is over, it's really over. Don't let failure control your life. You feel like kicking the tire. It's over. Things happen. Tough.

Did you know?

- Unser is a three-time Indy 500 champion ('68, '75 and '81).

- Dropped out of school after the 10th grade.

- Lifetime speeding tickets: "A lot less than most people think."

- Favorite eatery in Indianapolis: Steak 'n Shake. Orders a bowl of chili.

Stand up to bullies

Dan Vasella, Novartis CEO 1996-2010 on responding to activist scare tactics

✓ In 2009, animal rights activists went to my hometown village and painted "murderer" on the church. A week later, they desecrated the graves of my sister and parents. They set fire to my Austrian vacation home.

✓ Don't stay quiet. You have the duty as a citizen to speak up. If everyone remains silent, then violent people prevail.

✓ Security consultants say, don't respond, don't react. I say, be cool and react with logic. Be prudent, take precautions, but don't be afraid. Be willing to engage with activists such as Greenpeace – if they have a point. But not if their objective is to create fear and uncertainty. Those are terrorist attempts at psychological tension.

"Suffering in silence doesn't help anybody. Ducking to stay off the radar of negative publicity is a bad recipe."

- ✓ In minor instances it's best to stay quiet. It's a judgment call. Make a deliberate decision, not an emotional one.

- ✓ Encourage dialogue, but let activists know that criminal activity won't be tolerated.

- ✓ Visit activist websites to understand where they're coming from. If blackmail and extortion are their game, dialogue is useless. Don't win their support, win the public's support.

- ✓ If you go public, do it immediately. Engage politicians and the press.

- ✓ Take necessary security measures for your family.

- ✓ Remember what your parents said: Stand up for yourself.

Did you know?

- Vasella has an M.D. from the University of Bern in Switzerland.

- As a child, he had asthma, tuberculosis and meningitis and spent a year in a hospital/sanatorium.

- One sister died of Hodgkin's lymphoma at 19. Another sister, also a doctor, was killed in a car crash.

End a career with words of wisdom

Sandy Weill, Citigroup CEO 1998-2003 on selling a book

- ✓ Prepare for obvious questions. The most common one is: Why did you decide to write a book?

- ✓ Don't attempt a book unless you have something important to say. You have to open old wounds and criticisms.

- ✓ Ask yourself: Does my book have legs? Will people want to read it two years from now? Does it add value?

"If it's just something that's feathering your ego, shame on you."

- ✓ Don't use a book to settle grudges. Forgive. Learn about yourself.

- ✓ CEOs are competitive. You'll fear that the book will flop. Fear makes you pay more attention to what you're doing and makes you do better. Life is about overcoming fears and challenges – even once you're retired.

✓ Use a co-author who will write exactly the way you think and talk. Use the best and brightest. Don't be afraid if your co-author is brighter than you.

✓ Wait until you retire. It will be more work than you expect. You can't have a day job and write a book. Wait until you're ready. There may be chapters left unfinished.

"I never kept a diary during my career, but I would recommend it."

✓ Promote the book with hard work. You can't get on *Oprah*. Maybe you'll get *CSPAN*.

✓ Few interviewers will have read the book. Take their bad questions and convert them into something you want to say. Learn from politicians. Their answers have nothing to do with the question.

✓ The best way to move on to another question is to stop talking. Interviewers don't like dead air.

✓ The best way to combat an adversarial interview is to give long answers. Another lesson from politicians is the filibuster.

✓ Don't include an index. People will go to the back of the book, read their name and read the thing about themselves out of context. They won't read the rest.

✓ Let your wife write the last chapter. She made the trip with you. She contributed more than you'll know.

Did you know?

- Weill wrote *The Real Deal: My Life in Business and Philanthropy*. At 73, he did about 100 media interviews.

- Favorite books written by other business leaders: *Personal History* by Katherine Graham; *Iacocca* by Lee Iacocca. "Both are honest and self-critical."

Getting rid of the riffraff

Jack Welch, General Electric CEO 1981-2001 on scraping off the barnacles

- ✓ Rank all employees every year. The top 20% are stars. The bottom 10% are weeded out. It's called differentiation – or rank and yank.

- ✓ It's a lesson from the playground. The best get picked first.

- ✓ It's not cruel. The kindest thing is letting workers know where they stand. You give them a chance to improve or move on.

"Most leave on their own. Who wants to be on the bottom?"

- ✓ Suppose you've never been told you're on the bottom and along comes a downturn in the economy and you have to go. Differentiation is more honest.

"Is it kinder to never let anybody know their shortcomings and then surprise them with bad news?"

✓ Don't be rigid. You may get rid of 7% one year and 15% the next.

✓ Free time to nurture the winners and those who are growing. Take care of your very best. They won't react poorly to rank and yank. They recognize there are those who don't carry their load.

✓ When managers rank all employees, politics will creep into the system. Guard against that with an evaluation system that's as rigorous and fair as you can make it.

"I wanted to give hourly workers stock options, but the union said everyone had to get the same, which defeated the purpose."

✓ I agree with Larry Brown of the Detroit Pistons, a proponent of positive coaching. He says the best players are rewarded with the most money and adulation, but in the locker room and on the court they must act like part of the team.

188

Did you know?

- Welch was an altar boy. He once traveled more than an hour to attend mass, but when his mother died of a heart attack he got "angry and mad at God." He's a regular church-goer again.

- Will he go to heaven? He answers in his book, *Winning*: "I'm not perfect, but if there are any points given for caring about people with every fiber of your being and giving life all you've got every day, then I suppose I have a shot."

- Once beat professional Greg Norman over 18 holes. He's given up golf.

Quarterbacks play to win

Steve Young, 49er QB on the leadership lessons of football

- ✓ Business needs to play more hurry-up offense. Run a bunch of plays and more good things will happen. Huddle less in meetings.

- ✓ Offices should be open spaces. A locker room atmosphere breeds teamwork.

- ✓ A CEO is the combination of a QB and a coach. It takes both to get everyone headed in the right direction.

- ✓ Football has a score. You're in bounds, or you're out. Business doesn't have that, which makes it more difficult in many ways.

- ✓ Perfect information is never available. Gut instinct is crucial. Play a little blind, throw the ball trusting the receiver will be there. Take advantage of a glimpse, a piece of information.

- ✓ An element of faith is important.

"Even at six-foot-two I couldn't see my receivers over the defensive line. I knew Jerry Rice was there, I just couldn't see him. I let it rip. When I started playing essentially blind I accelerated my success."

✓ There's an element of luck, but never count on it. Even in a blizzard, the best team wins most of the time.

"Sound, practiced, accountable organizations win, and they win more when it gets crazy and tough."

✓ Call the play. Keep pushing forward. Don't finger-point. That's a defeatist attitude. Overcome everything and never flinch. There's always an excuse to make, but successful teams never open that door. It's true in football, business and families.

✓ If you make a mistake you say, "Fellas, I screwed up. I'm sorry, it won't happen again." They respond to that.

"If a leader isn't accountable, it breeds contempt."

✓ If someone else is at fault, don't lay blame on the field. When the battle is over, when things have quieted down, that's the time to look at the elements of a mistake.

✓ Everyone is driven by a fear of failure. Don't let it hold you back. A football team in hurry-up offense is often successful because it is about to lose, so it is no longer afraid to lose.

✓ On the other hand, the team in the lead is playing not to lose. It's playing scared, which is why big leads are blown.

✓ It helps to know that the competition is really with yourself and your team. Think: How great can we be?

Did you know?

• Young is the great-great-great grandson of Brigham Young.

• Was once a contestant on *Who Wants to Be a Millionaire*. He went out when he said a crucible is a vessel that can withstand high pressure. Correct answer: It withstands high heat.

• Lost a 3-point basketball shooting contest to *Family Matters* TV actor Jaleel White (Steve Urkel) during the 1993 NBA All-Star weekend.

Zig when they say zag

Edward Zore, Mutual Financial Network CEO 2001-10 on being counterintuitive

- ✓ Seinfeld was a TV show about nothing. It sounded crazy, but it worked.

- ✓ When oil prices are high, energy companies invest in exploration, auto companies invest in fuel efficiency. Those are the obvious choices and examples of zagging instead of zigging, which often prove to be disastrous.

- ✓ Being counterintuitive can be the dull path when others are going for the exotic. Being counterintuitive can mean being boring when everyone else is chasing the latest thing.

- ✓ Drive the counterintuitive approach down to the rank and file. Instill a culture where ideas are open to examination, where there's not a dumb question. Be open to people thinking differently.

✓ Don't always be counterintuitive. That makes you predictable, the opposite of counterintuitive.

✓ Never stop challenging your own beliefs – but don't give up on something old that remains relevant.

Did you know?

- Zore is a hunter and fisherman. Once considered becoming a forester.

- Recommends *Atlas Shrugged* that defends capitalism. It's a zig-when-they-say-zag novel because it was written by Ayn Rand, a woman born under socialism.

One-Question Afterward

If you had a son or daughter graduating from college or high school this year, what advice would you give to them?

Aflac CEO Dan Amos 1990-present

"I've spoken at a few university commencements, and my message is always pretty much the same. I tell graduates to find their treasure. By treasure, I'm not talking about money or material possessions. I'm talking about something in life that they're passionate about and pursue. That's the key to true happiness."

Sara Lee CEO Brenda Barnes 2005-2010

"Find something that you have a great passion for, as that will not only make you happy, it will also make you successful."

Lincoln National CEO Jon Boscia 1998-2007

"Don't worry about making a mistake — you're young and you have a lot of time to experiment."

Medtronic CEO Art Collins 2002-2008

"Choose a first-class school or place to work that will challenge you, and then surround yourself with bright, motivated people with integrity. Work hard, push your limits, never stop learning, and always remember to have some fun along the way. Careers and lives are made one building block at a time, from the foundation up."

Best Western CEO David Kong 2004-present

"Stay true to one's beliefs. In the next 10 years, be patient and build a solid foundation. Sometimes it's difficult to see people who don't work as hard, or are less talented, get ahead. Some people are luckier. It's OK. In the end, hard work and dedication pays handsome dividends."

1-800-Flowers.com founder Jim McCann

"Bring your youth to the table. It's an asset. Share your energy and excitement. It will cost you nothing extra to have a passionate personality. Find a way to share your unique perspective. You understand things about technology and culture that my generation only reads about. Use this to your advantage."

Mutual of Omaha CEO Dan Neary 2004-2015

"Focus on activities that give you the most satisfaction. There are many tools available to increase your awareness of how you are wired as an individual. Knowledge about your interpersonal characteristics may help guide you to careers that you would find the most rewarding."

Office Depot CEO Steve Odland 2005-2010

"Do the right thing. You know what it is. Don't just pick a career at which you're good. Pursue something that comes intuitively and that you love instinctively. Success will follow. If everyone's doing it, don't. Popularity wanes. Fame and fortune are fleeting. Reputation remains. How you treat others defines who you are."

Samsung Electronics of America CEO Dong-Jin Oh 2005-09

"Even in the technologically advanced world we live in, it is important to be hard-working and dedicate yourself to achieve success in both your career and life."

Real estate entrepreneur R. Donahue Peebles

"For a high school graduate, Take a trip to another country for two weeks and then take a summer job in an industry you are considering for a career. Prepare for surprises and disappointments and embrace both. To a college graduate, the adventure has begun and it's time to shift into high gear. Work hard and effectively. If at all possible, get a job in your dream field, even if the salary is less. If you can't get that job, don't give up, keep pushing. The most important word is perseverance. Most people give up before achieving their goals, often right before the finish line. You must be in the arena to compete."

Deloitte & Touche Tohmatsu CEO Jim Quigley 2007-2012

"Nearly half of all teens say they would act unethically to get ahead or make more money, if they knew for sure they would not get caught. I find this troubling, and would advise any graduate to make ethical behavior their cornerstone. The question is not, 'Will I get caught?' or even, 'Is it legal?' To be successful in business and in life, follow the higher standard of, 'Is it right?' The people who follow this standard live richer, fuller lives and achieve success that lasts."

Pep Boys CEO Jeffrey Rachor 2007-2008

"Master the art of communication. The ability to communicate effectively with people from all walks of life will differentiate you from most peers and position you for success in whatever endeavor or career path you pursue."

Sun Microsystems CEO Jonathan Schwartz 2006-2009

"One, always have a plan. It's OK to change the plan. It's not OK to show up without one. Two, pick bosses, not jobs. Three, the harder you work, the luckier you'll get."

Loews Hotel CEO Jonathan Tisch 1989-present

"Take a job, any job. It might not be exactly what you want, but you can learn from every experience, especially since we don't really know where we will end up."

About the Editor

Del Leonard Jones, CEO of Casey Strikes Out Publishing, lives near Washington D.C. with his wife Dianna. He has two grown children. He recently published his first historical novel, *The Cremation of Sam McGee*, set in the 1898 heyday of yellow journalism and the pitched battle between  newspaper moguls Joseph Pulitzer and William Randolph Hearst.

Jones writes and podcasts Q&As with CEOs who have advice to share. Those interested in having a Q&A published in *USA Today* and/or appear with legendary CEOs in the second edition of this book are invited to suggest a topic via his web site https://caseystrikesout.wixsite.com/website.

He is available to speak on a number of topics including leadership, and how today's changing journalism environment is both similar and dissimilar to the yellow journalism of the late 1890s.

Jones officiates high school and collegiate sports and is writing a second historical novel set in the dawn of professional baseball, inspired by the 1888 ballad Casey At the Bat and told from the umpire's point of view. He is taking a stab at humor with *Thursdays with Trump. All I Really Need To Know I Learned From the First Season of the Apprentice.*

About The Cremation of Sam McGee

Fake news is nothing new...

At the behest of newspaper mogul William Randolph Hearst, celebrated correspondent Jayson Kelley goes to Havana in 1898 to report on the escalating tensions in Cuba's bid for independence. Except most of his front-page stories are fabricated to spread warmongering propaganda and boost readership in journalism's 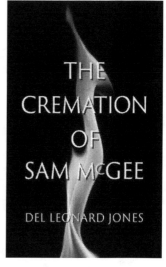 own circulation war at home. When Jayson meets Sam McGee and his beautiful but aloof sister Luisa, he knows he has his next story, crafting an unbelievable tale of heroism that leaves Sam dead and Luisa on the run. As the Spanish-American War unfolds, Jayson travels from the heat of Havana to the frozen Klondike at the height of the Gold Rush to fulfill an impossible promise he made to the best friend he's ever known and find the woman who stole his heart.

Based on the poems of Robert W. Service, Del Leonard Jones's debut novel is a richly-told historical fable about yellow journalism, fame, love, lies and redemption that *isn't too far* from the truth — and feels eerily believable in today's political climate, twenty-four-hour news cycle, and the cutthroat competition for clicks. *Sam McGee* is an epic battle for the high ground of honesty that continues to this day.

"*The Cremation of Sam McGee* reminds us again that history repeats itself. The language is stellar, the dialogue terrific, the characters larger than life. Jones does an incredible job."–T. Greenwood, author of *Rust & Stardust*.

Request the first chapter at
https://caseystrikesout.wixsite.com/website

Made in the USA
Lexington, KY
15 December 2019